THE COUNCIL OF CHIEF STATE SCHOOL OFFICERS
The Council of Chief State School Officers (CCSSO) is a nonpartisan, nationwide, nonprofit organization of public officials who head departments of elementary and secondary education in the states, the District of Columbia, the Department of Defense Education Activity, and five U.S. extra-state jurisdictions. CCSSO provides leadership, advocacy, and technical assistance on major educational issues. The Council seeks member consensus on major educational issues and expresses their views to civic and professional organizations, federal agencies, Congress, and the public.

THE ASSOCIATION OF TEST PUBLISHERS
The Association of Test Publishers (ATP) is a non-profit trade association for the international testing community, representing companies involved in developing and marketing assessments used in educational, organizational, clinical, and certification/licensure settings. ATP engages in federal and state advocacy efforts on behalf of the industry and provides educational activities for its members and users of assessments, including in the areas of professional development, intellectual property protection, test security, and emerging technology surrounding all forms of delivery, both paper and pencil and online.

COUNCIL OF CHIEF STATE SCHOOL OFFICERS
Steven Paine (West Virginia), President
Gene Wilhoit, Executive Director

Council of Chief State School Officers
One Massachusetts Avenue, NW, Suite 700
Washington, DC 20001-1431
Phone (202) 336-7000
Fax (202) 408-8072
www.ccsso.org

ASSOCIATION OF TEST PUBLISHERS
William G. Harris, Ph.D., Chief Executive Officer
Alan J. Thiemann, Counsel

601 Pennsylvania Avenue, NW
South Building, Suite 900
Washington, DC 20004
Phone (866) ?
Fax (717) 7!
www.testpubl

TECHNICAL
Daniel Eignc
Educational Test.

TABLE OF CONTENTS

INTRODUCTION TO *OPERATIONAL BEST PRACTICES*

Operational Best Practices for Statewide Large-Scale Assessment Programs

In June 2006, the Association of Test Publishers (ATP) and the Council of Chief State School Officers (CCSSO) began discussions to identify and publish a set of voluntary, non-regulatory best practices for states and testing companies to use to strengthen implementation of statewide testing programs in the United States conducted under the No Child Left Behind Act (NCLB). The original idea for developing a *Best Practices* guide actually originated in the U.S. Department of Education. This concept reflected a belief that such a document would facilitate quality testing practices for the benefit of everyone affected by state testing programs, including schools, parents, and students. Regardless of future legislative changes to the Elementary and Secondary Education Act (ESEA), states and testing companies will always find advantages from understanding what procedures help to form quality testing practices.

In December 2006, ATP and its testing company members agreed to form a best practices working group (WG) to review sample documents and to create a template for writing best practices that would be clear and useful to testing companies and states. Over the next eight months, the WG met numerous times and produced preliminary materials. CCSSO received periodic reports about this work, including a presentation at the Education Information Management Advisory Consortium (EIMAC) meeting in October 2007. Before the end of 2007, CCSSO agreed that representatives of the state assessment directors would join the WG and commence joint work to draft a formal document (*Operational Best Practices*). Since January, 2008, the expanded WG has worked diligently to develop this *Best Practices* document, which covers all major components of operating a large-scale state assessment program, from procurement to reporting test scores. The topics covered by the *Best Practices* are central to the tasks of designing, developing, administering, and scoring state assessments, and reporting state assessment results. Moreover, the operating practices described are considered to be reasonable and feasible, each having been reviewed carefully by both state assessment program leaders and testing industry veterans who are very familiar with the complexities of specific functions of state testing programs (e.g., program management, shipping of materials, test administration, etc.).

Inasmuch as the scope of the *Operational Best Practices* is limited to large-scale state assessment programs, the WG acknowledges that this document may not be precisely applicable to all testing protocols and systems, including those used on an international basis. Nevertheless, ATP and CCSSO believe that this document provides a solid framework from which others might seek to define a set of practices tailored to their testing programs; accordingly, ATP and CCSSO encourage others to use this document for that purpose. Moreover, the two organizations fully recognize that the testing process is not static; therefore, they expect that the *Best Practices* will be reviewed on a periodic basis, updated to account for changes in technology or testing methodologies (e.g., a growing reliance on online testing), to ensure that content remains viable.

This Introduction covers the following topics:

- **Sponsorship**
- **Criteria for Best Practices**
- **Development Procedures**
- **Review, Public Comments, and Final Adoption**
- **Use of the Document**
- **Terminology Used in the Document**

Sponsorship

This project is jointly sponsored by ATP, representing virtually all testing companies that currently provide services to state assessment programs, and CCSSO, including representatives of its state assessment directors group. Representatives of each organization participated fully in the development and review of the document. Going forward, publication and maintenance of these *Best Practices* will be undertaken by both ATP and CCSSO.

Criteria for Best Practices

In identifying and developing these *Operational Best Practices*, the WG applied several criteria to help ensure that the document describes proven practices that would provide concrete benefits to users. Each best practice had to:

- be directly related to the goal of enhancing operational test program quality, without conflicting with areas or principles specifically covered by scientific, professional technical standards embodied in the *Standards for Educational and Psychological Testing*;
- have a record of use by more than one state and/or testing company;
- be ready and available to be implemented by any testing company or state, without requiring, favoring, or advancing any particular technology choices to the detriment of others;
- be presented in a way that would permit alternative methods of attaining the same goal or objective; and
- be capable of being described through a measure related to its achievement or performance, rather than through specific requirements or prescribed steps or actions.

Only practices for which all participants agreed on their effectiveness were included. However, a consensus process was used for adoption of the substance and description of each practice.

Development Procedures

With overall guidance from ATP and CCSSO staff, the WG developed a plan for this project. Work on the project was accomplished through a series of face-to-face and telephone meetings to produce, review, and refine drafts. The sponsors wish to recognize the two co-Chairs of the Working Group, Jon Twing of Pearson, and Lisa Ehrlich of Measured Progress, for spending innumerable hours and providing leadership over the past two years of the project. The sponsors also gratefully acknowledge the following individual members of the WG who devoted substantial time and energy to the process:

- Wes Bruce, Indiana DOE
- Matthew Costello, The College Board
- Chris Domaleski, Georgia DOE
- Judy Feil, Ohio DOE
- John Fremer, Caveon Test Security
- Christopher Hanczrik, Washington Office of the Superintendent of Public Instruction
- Scott Hinders, Riverside Publishing
- Doyle Kirkeby, Data Recognition Corporation
- Dirk Mattson, Minnesota DOE
- Scott Merritt, CTB/McGraw-Hill
- Margaret Murphy, ETS
- Phil Young, ETS

The sponsors are deeply indebted to Daniel Eignor of ETS, who served as Editor for this project, for his expertise reviewing and analyzing the initial product as well as internal and external comments in crafting the final published product.

Review, Public Comments, and Final Adoption

From the outset of the project, the WG communicated with the testing industry and the states via written reports and presentations, including those at the ATP Annual Innovations in Assessment Conference, the EIMAC Conference, and the National Conference on Student Assessment.

Internal reviews of the *Best Practices* draft were conducted within ATP and CCSSO as well as multiple testing companies and state assessment staffs. The internal reviewers all had extensive experience with the various operational elements of designing and administering large-scale testing programs. Final reviews were managed by CCSSO, under the direction of first John Tanner and later Chris Minnich, with technical assistance from Joe Crawford. Use of an online management tool facilitated the gathering of reviews and allowed the WG to deal with a number of comments in refining the document into its final draft form.

Public comments on the final draft were collected from various stakeholders and potential users for a period of 60 days. Again, CCSSO's online management tool was utilized to collect and analyze both positive and negative public comments. A consensus process was employed by the WG to determine how to react to the comments. Once the WG completed its analysis of all public comments and made its final recommendations on revisions, the sponsors reviewed the entire package before adopting the final *Best Practices*.

Use of the Document

Several caveats accompany the publication of the final *Best Practices*; these are intended to guide readers in the proper use and interpretation of this document.

The sponsors seek to strengthen public confidence in the accuracy and quality of testing data and its uses in improving instruction and learning. The focus of these *Best Practices* is on specific operational testing practices that have the potential to enhance the quality, accuracy, and timeliness of student test data derived from large-scale state assessments. The document also recognizes the separate but interrelated and reciprocal responsibilities of testing companies and states in implementing state testing programs that meet the needs of both states and publishers.

These best practices are voluntary and are not part of any federal or state statutory or regulatory requirements, nor do the sponsors believe they should be. Moreover, implementation of these best practices by testing companies and states is not an "all or nothing" proposition. Successful testing programs have been created and administered without each practice being employed. In reality, some practices may not be applicable in some settings, for some states, under some circumstances. Accordingly, the sponsors wish to emphasize that successful testing programs may not need to incorporate each and every practice or each and every component of a practice.

The state assessment process is constantly evolving. Therefore, to facilitate review for the next version, the sponsors have adopted an online procedure for submitting feedback to the *Best Practices*. Further comments will be collected and considered by a new WG expected to begin its work in 2011.

Please share your comments to improve this document at: http://www.ccsso.org/best_practices_review/

Terminology Used in the Document

A glossary of terms used in the *Best Practices* is provided at the end of this document. However, because of the frequency and the manner in which the following four terms are used in the document, the Working Group thought it was important to provide definitions in the Introduction. The four terms are project manager, program manager, client, and service provider. The definition of how each of these terms is used in the document follows.

Project Manager: A project manager is the person assigned by the performing organization to achieve the project objective. According to the Program Management Institute (PMI), a project is a temporary endeavor undertaken to create a unique product, service, or result. For a statewide assessment, a project manager is generally responsible for the delivery of one or more components of an assessment contract.

Program Manager: A program manager is the person assigned to coordinate and manage all elements of the program. According to PMI, a program is a group of related projects managed in a coordinated way to attain benefits and control not available from managing them individually. For a statewide assessment, program managers for both the client and the service provider will be jointly responsible for the delivery of all components of an assessment contract.

Client:	A client is the entity which contracts for service. When applied in the large-scale assessment market, the client is typically a state department of education.
Service Provider:	A service provider is the entity which provides services to the client. When applied in the large-scale assessment market, a service provider contracting directly with the client is typically considered to be a prime contractor, which is called contractor in this document. Other service providers contracting with the prime contractor to provide components of the overall contract are typically considered to be subcontractors, which is the term used in this document.

CHAPTER 1. PROGRAM MANAGEMENT AND CUSTOMER SERVICE

Introduction

The use of proven program management best practices is central to the successful implementation of a statewide assessment program. The role of the service provider's program manager is to ensure that all products, services, related materials, and documentation ("deliverables") specified in the contract are of high quality, meet customer requirements, and are delivered on schedule and within budget. The equally important role of the client's program manager is to oversee all aspects of the contract from the client's perspective, to ensure that the program development is functioning smoothly and efficiently, and to respond to questions from the service provider's program manager.

To effectively create and operate a statewide assessment program, the client must develop a collaborative partnership between the client's program manager and the service provider's program manager. Both managers should coordinate core components of an effective program management approach. This will ensure that all requirements of the client's program are met. These requirements should include, at a minimum, agreed-upon processes and protocols for:

- scope definition and client requirements;
- costs;
- program transitioning;
- communication, meetings, and status reporting;
- scope change control;
- staffing changes; and
- expectations for working with the Local Education Agencies (LEAs) within a state.

Additional components may be added with the agreement of both parties.

The use of program management best practices in these areas should help ensure the implementation and administration of a successful quality program, a program that meets all stakeholders' expectations.

1.1 The service provider and the client will each appoint an individual to serve as its program manager. The duties of the program managers for each party include the following:

- overseeing the full scope of the program;

- overseeing the budget and invoicing process, which includes initiation and oversight for scope changes;

- developing and communicating procedures and protocols;

- addressing potential problems and promptly resolving existing problems;

- developing agenda topics for all meetings involving both parties;

- developing an agreed upon schedule for all deliverables;

- ensuring all timelines and milestones are met;

- establishing and implementing the chain of decision-making within both parties;

- ensuring clear communication between both parties at all levels; and

- ensuring all deliverables required under the contract are accurate, complete, and timely.

1.2 The program managers for the service provider and the client should have a clear understanding of the scope and costs of the program. The program managers should have an understanding about the contract requirements. They should disclose any issues that may jeopardize the success of the program.

1.3 Program managers for the client and the service provider should work collaboratively and establish a team approach.

1.4 A process should be established for identifying the required program management qualifications for each segment of the contractual requirements.

1.4.1 Both the service provider and the client should prepare a list of required qualifications for their program managers and jointly review these lists. Qualifications should address the following:

- certification(s) required;

- educational background and experience required;

- other experience required (e.g., experience dealing with special populations/subgroups); and

- experience required in meeting unique client specifications.

1.4.2   Based on the qualifications above, the service provider and client should identify their respective program managers.

1.5   A program planning meeting with key client and service provider staff should be conducted before starting a new program. Program transitions may require meetings prior to the initial meeting. It is strongly recommended that subsequent meetings occur at least semi-annually.

1.5.1   Agendas for meetings should be developed jointly by the service provider and the client. The agenda for each meeting should include the following:

- discussion points related to the current deliverables and milestones;

- updates to key staff assignments and changes in responsibilities;

- new issues arising since the last meeting; and

- any other information or issues related to the program managers' duties.

1.5.2   A set of specifications for meeting logistics should be developed.

1.5.3   Minutes of each meeting should be kept and provided to all participants in a timely fashion.

1.5.4   Documentation of the scope of work and program specification requirements should be developed and made available to all attendees. This documentation should include the following:

- annual program schedule;

- service provider milestones;

- specified key dates;

- roles and responsibilities of key staff;

- materials list associated with milestones;

- list of deliverables and handoffs associated with milestones; and

- evaluation of previous project implementation, outstanding issues, and/or a risk analysis plan, including mitigation activities, if applicable.

1.5.5   The client should provide program information and requirements. Both the service provider and the client should agree upon a schedule for delivery of products, services, and documentation. This documentation should include specifications for provision of the following:

- student background and demographic information;

- student enrollment information;

- school addresses and relevant school information;

- district database information including addresses, and relevant staff and contact information; and

- school database information and class assignments.

1.6   Protocols should be established between the client and the service provider to help ensure communication between the parties. These protocols should address the following:

- chain of decisions;

- status reports;

- planning agendas;

- meeting minutes;

- conference calls at set intervals;

- milestone meetings or other meetings at set intervals as specified by contract; and

- scope changes.

1.7 A separate protocol may need to be developed to identify changes to the scope and/or schedule of the original contract and to determine how the revised scope should be managed from both fulfillment (service/delivery) and business perspectives.

1.7.1 Identification of any change in scope that requires a contract modification should be the responsibility of both the client and the service provider.

1.7.2 Program management staff (for both the service provider and the client) should discuss the scope change and seek agreement and approval of a new scope of work.

1.7.3 If a change request is made and the client and the service provider agree upon a new or changed scope of work, the service provider should present the client with a written proposal or addendum to the contract setting forth terms of the new scope of work. This proposal/addendum should include information on the following:

- any changes in deliverables or new deliverables;

- any modifications or updates to schedule; and

- all costs associated with change request.

1.7.4 The client should approve the service provider's proposal before work commences, subject to terms of the contract.

1.7.5 If extenuating circumstances require that work begin before a scope change process can be completed, a "work-at-risk protocol" should be put into place. This protocol should describe how work can be started prior to contract adjustments and clearly articulate risks and responsibilities for all parties involved. If state procurement law prohibits "work-at-risk," that limitation needs to be communicated to the service provider and its impact clearly explained.

1.8   A procedure for handling staffing changes required by the service provider will be developed with, and agreed upon, by the client. To the extent possible, adequate notice should be given so that the search for a replacement can commence in a timely fashion.

    1.8.1   A procedure should be established for dealing with the situation where a key staff member becomes unavailable to serve the program. This could occur for many reasons, including an employee leaving the service provider, taking medical leave, or changing job status. This procedure should address the following:

- the process for identifying an individual's replacement;

- the procedures for early and full disclosure regarding communication of any replacements; and

- the plan to help ensure replacement meets all qualifications of position and is integrated into program as soon as possible, preferably with some overlap, to provide a smooth transition.

    1.8.2   A plan for documentation and key resource transfer should be developed to help ensure a smooth transfer of personnel for either the client or the service provider.

1.9   The client will work with the service provider to establish and maintain a working relationship with the schools and districts within the state. This relationship should include protocols for:

- communication (e.g., who contacts districts to follow up on any identified action);

- distribution, administration, and collection of materials; and

- creation of a customer service and support help desk.

1.10   The service provider will update the client with progress reports that are timely and well documented. The client will notify the service provider in advance, to the extent possible, of any extenuating circumstances that might cause delays.

1.11 The service provider will manage and be responsible for all subcontractors it uses for the program.

1.12 Processes will be established to help ensure the accuracy, reliability, and validity of information provided to clients or school/district representatives by customer service and program support representatives.

    1.12.1 Quality assurance methods for customer service and support should be developed to help ensure accuracy of information.

    1.12.2 Ongoing training of customer service representatives should be conducted to help ensure they possess the most up-to-date information.

    1.12.3 Processes should be established to help ensure consistent messaging regarding products, procedures, and processes if/when multiple customer service and support representatives are communicating with clients or school/district representatives.

1.13 Processes will be established to help ensure client orders are processed accurately and in a timely manner.

    1.13.1 A process for tracking uncompleted orders, client requests, or issues should be established and provided on a daily or regular basis to customer service and program support management to help ensure that client-related issues are not neglected.

    1.13.2 A document retention process should be created for orders, client requests, or issues that are received online or via fax, e-mail, or USPS.

    1.13.3 Such documents should be reviewed on a daily basis by customer service and support representatives to determine any order, client request, or issue that can be, or has been, solved or corrected.

1.14 Processes will be established to facilitate an orderly transition of verbal or written communication from the customer service or support system to other departments within the service provider's organization.

1.15 Processes will be established to help ensure that material and communication security is enforced and confidentiality maintained. This is especially important when resolving issues related to materials on secure materials lists or issues involving student identification information or individual student results.

1.16 Customer service or support functions may not always follow the service provider's standard processes. This divergence may be due to unique client requirements as articulated in the contract or Request for Proposal (RFP) process. In such cases, processes should be established for identifying staffing requirements and modifications necessary to meet client needs.

   1.16.1 The client should inquire about how to best leverage and use the service provider's existing customer service and support processes.

   1.16.2 Using existing services should yield economies of scale and make the best use of cumulative history and experience of the service provider.

1.17 A post-program review meeting should be conducted documenting lessons learned and improvement plans.

CHAPTER 2. ITEM DEVELOPMENT

Introduction

An assessment cycle should begin with clearly defined test specification documents that enable the development of test items. These specifications define the item types (multiple choice, short answer, open response, performance task, etc.), grade level, and content coverage based on the state's or program's curriculum standards. Using well-defined test specifications, items are developed by the service provider and reviewed through processes adopted by the client, including using universal design principles so that, to the extent feasible, items are developed for all student populations (e.g., all student subgroups, including students with disabilities and English Language Learners (ELLs)).

2.1 **Test specifications describing attributes of the assessment should be developed for each grade and content area prior to the development of assessment items and related ancillary materials.**

2.1.1 The client should provide the service provider with the state academic content standards along with the corresponding curricular frameworks and benchmarks. The client should also provide the service provider with the measurement specifications, the passage or stimulus selection guidelines, the existing performance level descriptors, and if used, the style guide, prior to the beginning of development activities.

2.1.2 The service provider and the client should define the details of the test specifications. These specifications should include the following:

- the test design (number of items, formats of items, number of passages/stimuli, desired layouts, use of supporting materials like calculators, etc.);

- the need, if any, for alternative assessment forms or alternate assessments for special populations;

- the test curriculum blueprint for each grade and content area (coverage of curriculum frameworks and benchmarks, often manifested as a percentage of test items per standard or benchmark); and

- the item development plan (process for development of test items, typically including item prototypes, process for passage acquisition, definition of item development specifications, consideration of the client's accommodations policy and/or allowable accommodations, item review procedures, schedules, quantities, and quality acceptance criteria).

2.1.3   The service provider and the client should define the details of item specifications. Item specifications may include the following:

- content to be tested;

- item type(s) to be employed;

- intended level of cognitive complexity;

- intended level of difficulty;

- reading level of reading passages;

- attendance to varying levels of student achievement;

- suitability of access for special populations; and

- use of graphics, tables, charts, etc.

2.2   A timeline for the development of test items should be established and agreed upon by the service provider and the client.

2.2.1   Revisions to the timeline should be agreed upon by the service provider and client.

2.2.2   The agreed-upon timeline should be adhered to by both parties.

2.3   The service provider will specify an internal item development process, including editorial procedures. This process should cover the following:

- development of items by individuals with expertise in the content area for which items are being developed;

- multiple rounds of internal reviews;

- sensitivity reviews;

- the level of accessibility for special populations and possible allowable accommodations; and

- editorial reviews.

2.4 The service provider may want to procure an external, independent review of specifications and items depending upon the agreement reached between the service provider and the client.

2.5 The service provider should conduct internal reviews of draft items prior to their final adoption, checking for the following:

- alignment to standards and curricular frameworks derived from content standards;

- alignment to appropriate level of cognitive complexity;

- compliance with item specifications;

- accuracy of keyed response;

- reasonableness and completeness of scoring rubrics for constructed response (CR) items;

- grade appropriateness;

- accuracy and completeness of diagrams, tables, graphics, etc.;

- editorial appropriateness;

- sensitivity issues;

- level of accessibility for special populations, possible allowable accommodations; and

- appropriateness of alternative assessment forms or alternate assessments for use by special populations where allowable accommodations may not be available.

2.6 **Iterative rounds of revisions and rewrites may occur with the service provider and the client, tracking the status of the items.**

2.7 **The service provider and the client will jointly facilitate reviews, including the following, when necessary/appropriate:**

- item content review committee meetings;

- sensitivity committee review meetings; and

- other reviews.

2.8 **The client will identify members of each review committee and/ or the requirements the service provider will follow for soliciting and securing appropriate committee members. Committees may be convened by grade and content area or committees might include multiple grades and/or multiple content areas.**

2.8.1 Requirements for committee selection, process for securing committee members, and results of such a process should be documented when appropriate, including the following:

- target committee attributes, if known or desired;

- relevant demographics, and other committee selection characteristics (e.g., school district or constituency represented by committee member); and

- comparison of final committee makeup against any relevant target goals, including notation of differences, if any.

2.8.2 The service provider should furnish item analysis information to the client and review committees as agreed upon by contract. When sample size permits, such data should be provided for appropriate subgroups, including special populations. Item analysis information may include:

- response option distributions;

- percentile analysis (e.g., quartile analysis);

- item discrimination information (e.g., biserial correlations);

- proportion correct data; and

- Differential Item Function (DIF).

2.8.3   The number of committee meetings required or desired should be identified. Both the client and the service provider should work to ensure that costs, schedule, security procedures and requirements for committee meetings are part of the contract, statement of work, or RFP.

2.8.4   The service provider and the client should reach an agreement on who will facilitate committee meetings and how they will be facilitated.

2.8.5   Specific roles and responsibilities of staff from both the client and the service provider should be determined prior to committee meetings. These roles and responsibilities should be documented and communicated.

2.8.6   Contingency plans should be developed. These should include procedures that the client or service provider staff can follow in event of a committee meeting disruption (e.g., power outage, fire drill, or other unforeseen facility issue), disruptive committee member, security breach when secure materials are being reviewed, failure of committee or staff members to attend the meeting, or errors in printed materials.

2.8.7   Expense reimbursement and honorarium payment procedures should be established, documented, and communicated to the client and the service provider staff as well as to committee members.

2.8.8   Materials for committee review, facility logistics, and check-in/verification procedures should be established and distributed ahead of time.

2.8.9   For site-based review, meeting rooms should be arranged to optimize committee interaction. When possible, non-secure materials should be distributed within meeting rooms prior to committee arrival.

2.8.10　For virtual reviews, the technology requirements should be distributed to the committee participants prior to the meeting. Support should be made available to participants for access during meeting.

2.9　The client will specify program requirements for passages, written materials, graphics, photographs, and other related item stimuli. These requirements will determine the need for permissions and rights solicitations. These requirements should include:

- use of authentic versus commissioned materials;

- administration details for field and/ or operational testing;

- posting on the internet for release following an assessment; and

- paper-based or online assessment presentations.

2.10　The client and the service provider will define an item review process and acceptance criteria. This process should cover the following areas:

- client review prior to committee review;

- committee and/or department review protocols;

- post-committee protocols;

- version control of items by the service provider as items move through review;

- item bank analysis by the service provider to determine areas of needed item/passage development before new development begins, although the client may conduct its own analysis, with results shared between both parties;

- the service provider updating the client on the acceptance rate of items; and

- other processes identified by the parties.

CHAPTER 3. ITEM BANKING

Introduction

An item bank is a repository for crucial information regarding many aspects of an assessment program. This information is used for item evaluation, test form construction, legal defensibility, and planning for future item development efforts. Such a repository often contains more than just test items. An item bank may also contain stimulus materials, artwork, statistical data, administration history, or other "meta" data that allow for the linking of test items and their disposition to many other aspects of the assessment program, including the client's accommodation policy.

Often people speak of an "item bank" as if it was one central place for storing everything associated with assessment construction. While this may be true conceptually, it is seldom true in practice. Typically, an "item bank" is a compilation of many disparate, but linked, systems that work together to keep track of assessment items and associated collateral information. For example, artwork associated with a test item might "live" in one system in a location separate from the text of the test item itself. Similarly, the statistical data might "live" in yet another separate location but be linked to the test item in a number of ways. Finally, information regarding fonts, formats, and other attributes of test items (meta-data) might be located in yet another part of the system. Therefore, keeping track of these linked pieces of information is paramount in maintaining a successful program. During times of transition, the disposition of these assets must be known and understood for the appropriate hand-offs from the previous service provider to the new service provider or from one generation of department staff to another.

This chapter outlines some of the considerations regarding practices for establishing and maintaining linked assessment information, or item banks, that are likely to lead to successful use in an assessment program.

3.1 The item banking system should consist of the following:

- clear links with delineated paths to all items, passages, or other stimuli, art and graphics, and other required meta-data;

- clear links with delineated paths to other supportive documents, such as:

  - scoring rubrics, criteria, or directions;

  - information on allowable accommodations;

  - pre-testing collateral such as checklists or pre-organizers; and

  - required manipulatives;

- attributes of the assessment items, such as:

  - item cluster, objective, or sub-domain memberships;

  - information about shared passages, stimuli, graphics, artwork, or other similar linkages;

  - cloned items or other item-to-item dependencies, such as items that can not appear in the same form of the test;

  - distribution rationales; and

  - calculator designation;

- alignment information, such as:

  - curriculum, content standards, and benchmarks an item (and associated collateral) measures; and

  - depth of test-taker knowledge required by item or other non-content related classification taxonomy;

- disposition, parameters, and attributes of items, stimuli, passages, and tasks, such as:

  - the item use history;

  - the date when item was constructed;

- the correct answer key, prototypical response set for open-ended or free-response items;

- a clearly delineated link to rights and permissions for artwork, passages, or graphics;

- the committee comments, reviews, actions, and/or recommendations;

- the statistical data from field test, and all operational, uses of the item;

- the item positioning within test booklet (sequencing) for all operational uses of the item;

- the information regarding public release, including release date for items, passages, and all items associated with a passage if not in the original release;

- the expert reviewer comments, if provided for by contract, such as third-party review of the use of universal design principles or item alignment findings;

- the items not yet field tested but approved, as well as approved but untested reading passages, stimuli, and graphics (including original source file), or when this is not possible, clearly delineated item banking system links to the location of the passages, stimuli, and graphics should be established and documented;

- the items, attributes, and systems appropriately linked to allow for electronic creation of an item card at any stage that contains item image and attributes; and

- the systems appropriately linked to facilitate operational item selection that ensures accurate information;

- clear links to the relevant information on the following types of assessments:

  - portfolio assessments and their collateral;

  - online, CAT, or CBT assessments;

  - alternative assessment forms or alternate assessments for students with disabilities; and

  - assessments for English Language Learners (ELLs) and in the case of tests delivered in languages other than English, a clear link to the English language source, particularly if the source resides in the same item banking system.

3.2 The item bank should be made available to the client, when required.

3.2.1 Procedures and processes for item bank use by the client (and any subcontractors of the service provider) should be established and documented as part of contract. The following areas should be covered:

- technology requirements;

- item format disposition at the end of the contract (e.g., XML format, PDF format, or other accessible formats when the item bank is the proprietary custody of the service provider); and

- training needs, schedules, and procedures.

3.2.2 Procedures and processes for item bank security when used by the client (and any subcontractors of the services provider) should be established and documented as part of the contract.

3.3 Maintenance of the item bank should be the responsibility of the service provider with oversight by the client.

3.3.1 Roles and responsibilities regarding maintenance of the ongoing item banking system should be established.

3.3.2　A schedule and procedures for routine item bank maintenance (importing of data, items, or other stimuli) should be established, agreed upon by both the client and service provider, and should include the following:

- when and how new content, data, standards, or other rules of the assessment program will be added to the item banking system;

- a schedule of item disposition to the client, if it is not at the end of the contract (e.g., yearly transfer of items to the client if property of the client, as defined in contract); and

- version control processes to help ensure appropriate links to meta-data.

3.3.3　The item bank should be maintained in a controlled, secure environment and should adhere to all applicable security requirements agreed upon by the client and the service provider, or as set forth elsewhere in this document.

3.3.4　The item bank should be accessible through a secure format from remote locations rather than solely from installed computers at the client's site.

CHAPTER 4. TEST BOOKLET CONSTRUCTION AND DEVELOPMENT

Introduction

Once the item development cycle is completed, new operational items are selected (including items for common item equating and for embedded field testing within the assessment forms). All items must also comply with test specifications, form layout, and appropriate psychometric considerations. Test specifications are developed and reviewed annually. Using identified selection criteria, the client reviews and approves the selected new, common, and embedded field test items, usually in collaboration with the service provider staff.

Production of assessment materials begins once the final items have been selected. Test forms are laid out on each page using agreed-upon production guidelines and protocols. In concert with the test booklet production, associated scannable answer documents are developed and constructed. The layout of the item response sections for answer documents follows the item flow of the test booklets, using agreed-upon labeling of multiple choice response areas and allotting answer space for short answer and constructed response items as defined in the test specifications. For items requiring ancillary manipulatives, the specifications for these are defined during the test development process and approved by the client and then are developed during the production cycle.

Requirements for special forms are defined by program needs and by the client. These may include Braille forms, large print forms, forms in languages other than English, CDs, DVDs, videotapes, and other usable formats. The items contained in these forms are also specified by the program. To the extent feasible, these forms should be developed at the same time as the targeted main assessment form.

4.1 **Procedures, processes, responsibilities, and timelines should be established and implemented for selecting operational items, passages, graphics, artwork, stimulus materials, manipulatives, or other assessment collateral.**

4.1.1   Because of rights and permissions issues, selection of passages, artwork, or graphics may need to be conducted early in the process. Regardless of when it is conducted, procedures, processes, and responsibilities should be clearly delineated and documented.

4.1.2   Procedures, processes, responsibilities, and timelines for review, verification and approval of content selection using test development specifications should be established and implemented. These procedures should cover the following:

- identification of the number of reviews or stages of review;

- identification of reviewers from the client's staff, the service provider's staff, and/or others;

- specification of the chain of authority regarding required and documented approval signatures;

- identification of procedures to help ensure security during review and approval process; and

- determination of action plans for when items or other selected content are not approved and must be replaced, including schedule impacts and risk assessment.

4.1.3   Specifications should include procedures and processes describing how to develop multiple forms for assessments that contain a core or common set of items, if applicable, along with many different versions or forms containing embedded field-test questions, including alternative forms. Procedures should include specifications for how forms of a test containing field-test items, as defined by test development specifications, are constructed. These procedures should ensure that:

- all test forms follow the same blueprint;

- all test forms have a similar "look and feel;"

- items used on all assessment forms are piloted and/or field tested in the format in which they will be used; and

- items that were rejected or released are not included on the forms.

4.1.4 Test construction procedures should specify the statistical models to be employed in the process.

4.1.5 The following factors should be considered when specifying the layout of answer documents:

- positioning of demographic data as defined by data requirements;

- test taker characteristics and ability to select/ use answer sheet formats (e.g., age and membership in special populations);

- margins, marks, and image capture requirements as specified in scanning documents;

- section breaks to match test booklet layout;

- for combined test booklet/answer documents, appropriate space provided for handwritten responses; and

- the functional layout to minimize gridding errors.

4.2 Procedures will be developed for coordinating test booklet production, the selection of test items, the generation of multiple forms, and the physical production of the test booklets (either in paper-based or online format). These procedures should include:

- requirements of materials manufacturing as outlined elsewhere in this document;

- schedules for the review of materials that have been developed in collaboration with others in determining materials manufacturing;

- agreed-upon formatting, layout (including font and white space requirements), and style guide requirements as determined by procedures outlined in other sections of this document;

- agreed-upon procedures, processes, and timelines for review of final test booklets (online or print-based) early enough in the production cycle to accommodate any identified defects; and

- agreed-upon procedures, processes, timelines, and requirements for generating supporting or ancillary material such as administrator manuals and other collateral.

4.3 Test form development will be a joint effort of the service provider and the client.

4.4 A timeline for test form development, reviews, modifications, and approval will be developed and agreed upon by the service provider and client.

4.4.1 Both parties should commit to a well-defined timeline.

4.4.2 Both parties should agree on any changes to the timeline.

4.4.3 Any unexpected delays by either the service provider or client should be communicated to the other party as soon as delay is evident.

4.5 The service provider will provide the client with information to use in the review and approval process as set forth in the contract. Such information should include the following:

- the items selected for the operational form along with the agreed-upon item statistics;

- the first formatted version of test booklets;

- the final version of test booklets prior to production;

- the formatted version of the test booklets with embedded field test items, if applicable;

- the final version of answer documents,

including demographic data collection as defined by program requirements;

- the associated manuals; and

- the final copy of all special versions, which may include Braille versions and large print versions, versions in languages other than English, English audio versions, and scripts for read-aloud and translations.

4.6   The service provider will provide the client with all relevant information about the proposed test form, along with information on each iteration of changes made to the form, as set forth in the contract. The client will use this information to review and approve the test form. This information may include:

- average difficulty of the test form;

- distribution of difficulties across the form;

- balance of items that may contain any DIF;

- scoring key and alignment information; and

- prior parameter estimates for common items to be used in form equating.

CHAPTER 5. STAND-ALONE FIELD TESTING

Introduction

In instances where it is not desirable to embed field test items within an operational assessment, a separate independent "stand-alone" field test is necessary. Such instances include, for example, when student fatigue is a concern with the operational assessment or when new item types need to be field tested. The goal of administering this field test is to collect performance statistics on items/writing prompts used to inform the later selection of operational assessment items. The decision to conduct these field tests within client's state, outside the state, and/or with a specific cohort of test-takers, rather than embed the field test items within an operational form, is a result of a number of factors. Some considerations include:

- Security — writing prompts and performance tasks involve security issues because they are typically memorable;
- Timing of contract administration — there are instances when it is "too late" in a particular assessment cycle to conduct an embedded field test, or when an entirely new testing program is beginning;
- Operational attributes — administration constraints dictate the test/session length, precluding the incorporation of embedded field test items;
- High stakes testing — defensibility of embedding field-test items in a high stakes assessment;
- Test design — testing or psychometric decisions require everyone to only take the same set of items; and
- Special populations — need to try out items to see how they work with special populations.

5.1 **The following field test elements should be defined and mutually agreed upon by the client and the service provider:**

    5.1.1   Field test specifications should be defined in such a way as to yield a balance in the required number of items needed later for operational administration by item type and by requirements for content coverage as defined by specifications.

5.1.2   The number of field test forms and individual form layouts should be defined to produce the required yield (number of items) and to satisfy necessary administration requirements (e.g., there may need to be multiple sessions of field testing to match operational administration needs). The number of field test forms is not independent of the total number of test-takers that can be tested.

5.1.3   The participation guidelines should be defined and distributed as part of solicitation communications.

5.1.4   The schedule for administration, scoring, and analysis work should be created.

5.2   The following field test procedures for special populations should be agreed upon by the client and the service provider:

5.2.1   Field tests for alternative assessment formats (e.g., Braille, large print) should be conducted using only students within each targeted subgroup or special population.

5.2.2   Field testing involving special populations should occur with students receiving the appropriate accommodations allowed for the particular assessment form used or to determine the appropriateness of proposed accommodations (e.g., individual student IEPs and/or 504 plans).

CHAPTER 6. MANUFACTURING OF TEST MATERIALS

Introduction

Best practices for manufacturing test materials involve or include systems and procedures that ensure appropriate material types and volumes. This includes overage created in accordance with client requirements. Proper checks and balances must be put in place to ensure that materials are properly printed, sequenced, and assembled, and that they facilitate efficient and accurate use by the client. This process also must be easily replicable to account for separate accommodations materials as well as client requests for extra materials or breach forms.

6.1   **All test materials should meet contract specifications and the service provider's processing and scanning requirements.**

    6.1.1   All materials should be controlled in a manner that ensures:

- product specifications are met;
- technical specifications for form, fit, and function are achieved;
- quality acceptance criteria are achieved; and
- traceability and record retention are maintained.

    6.1.2   Materials critical to the successful capture and scoring of the assessment program should be controlled for, including:

- correct stock;
- correct ink;
- scanning indicators (where applicable);
- completeness and accuracy; and
- storage and handling requirements.

6.2   **A process should be established and approved by the service provider and the client to help ensure production of necessary quantities of manufactured materials based upon enrollment data and overage requirements provided by the client.**

6.2.1   This process should include a way to estimate the materials required at the testing site. This process could include developing an algorithm for estimating the overall quantity of materials needed.

6.2.2   Information to begin this process may come from student enrollment and participation databases (see 18.2.2).

6.2.3   A specifications document that includes a materials list should be developed. This document should delineate all of the material requirements, including a plan for additional orders of materials that may be requested.

6.2.4   A document containing specific quantities for all materials including recommended overage and special forms (i.e., Braille, large print, forms in languages other than English, and other special materials) should be produced.

6.3   A process should be established to help ensure that all test materials meet specifications prior to final production. The quality assurance process should include checks during printing.

6.4   A process should be established to help ensure accurate collating of test materials. The collating process should include a page-signature verification system or related system, which could employ bar code readers, and/or operator checklists and spot checks.

6.5   A process should be established to identify secure materials.

6.5.1   A specifications document should be created that defines security requirements such as the placement of a unique security code, size, configuration, and read requirements as delineated in other sections of this document.

6.5.2   A process should be established to account for and replace secure materials that may be damaged as a part of the production process.

6.6   A process should be established, where required, to pre-code answer documents with state-assigned unique student identification and demographic information, LEA and school/ testing site codes, etc.

6.6.1   The client should provide an electronic data file that contains the most current student identification, demographic, and score attribution information available to allow for the accurate administration, scoring, and reporting of standardized tests.

6.6.2 The service provider should work closely with the client to define required data elements and to determine schedules and procedures for the transfer of electronic pre-code data.

6.6.3 The service provider should work closely with the client to define a process to manage changes to the pre-code data file.

6.6.4 Human-readable information should be on the barcode label or preprinted on the answer document. This should provide enough information to match the answer document to the appropriate student.

6.6.5 A unique barcode should be printed on the answer document, which will link to the electronic student data file.

6.7 A process should be established to ensure all materials, including accommodations materials, are spiraled, if necessary, and then shrink-wrapped, banded, or packaged according to the contract specifications.

6.7.1 The spiraling process should include quality checks to help ensure accuracy, and could employ:

- bar code readers; and/or

- operator checklists.

6.7.2 Shrink-wrapped or banded packages should have clear identification of contents. This should be completed by using:

- example range sheets;

- visible first and last documents; and

- content description labels.

6.7.3 A process should be determined for production of extra materials, if need arises, including production of breach forms and associated materials.

6.7.4 The plan for production of extra materials should be developed and agreed upon by the client and service provider.

CHAPTER 7. THIRD-PARTY MANAGEMENT

Introduction

Service providers often engage outside parties to fulfill component projects of a statewide testing program. These third-party subcontractors can be vendors, freelancers, or consultants who may or may not be named in a service provider's proposal. In all instances, management best practices will apply to the service provider and all such third-parties to ensure adherence to contractual obligations; however, the service provider is ultimately responsible for the deliverables from the third party.

7.1   The client may establish requirements for the use of third-party providers. Examples may include the use of in-state providers, minority-owned businesses, women-owned businesses, and major subcontractors added after the contract is awarded.

7.2   A third party may or may not be named in the service provider's proposal to the client.

   7.2.1   When a third party is named, it should be designated as a subcontractor with responsibility for specific project work to be delivered.

   7.2.2   Unnamed third parties providing services are typically vendors, freelancers, or consultants. These third-party providers usually provide a commoditized service and it is the service provider's responsibility to ensure these entities adhere to the contract.

7.3   The service provider has a responsibility to the client to ensure that the third party (named or unnamed) delivers on the agreed-upon requirements. In order to help ensure that the contractual obligations are met, the service provider should:

   • establish confidentiality agreements and non-disclosure agreements;

   • ensure preparation of contracts for services and necessary work orders;

- define the scope of work to be delivered by the third party;

- document, agree upon, and institute a Service Level Agreement, that includes the scope of work, quality expectations, and turnaround of services;

- define program management expectations; and

- establish communication and escalation protocols.

7.4 **The third-party has a direct responsibility to the service provider and indirectly to the client through the service provider. The third-party provider should:**

- provide a letter of commitment if named as a subcontractor or if required by client; and

- designate a project manager or other point-of-contact responsible for third-party deliverables.

CHAPTER 8. SECURITY

Introduction

The validity, fairness, and integrity of state test results are dependent upon maintaining the security of the items and tests as well as the answer documents and certain ancillary materials that result from test administrations. This chapter discusses best practices for paper-and-pencil administrations. While many of these best practices also may apply in an online setting, a future chapter that addresses specific online security concerns is planned for the next edition of the *Operational Best Practices*. The cooperation of the service provider and the client is essential, as are the efforts of the teachers and others at school sites who receive, distribute, and return materials. The overall effectiveness of the effort requires careful planning and communication. This chapter addresses:

- **Security plans;**
- **Security training materials and agreements;**
- **Dealing with security breaches;**
- **Test administration security issues; and**
- **Protecting secure materials at all stages of distribution, storage, and return.**

8.1 **A comprehensive plan to help ensure the security of intellectual property (e.g., software, passages, items, test forms, other materials), data, electronic information, and assessment results will be developed, agreed upon, and implemented by the service provider and the client.**

    8.1.1 The security plan should establish and document rules for storage of secure materials.

    8.1.2 Rules and procedures to ensure security of materials during test construction, production, and processing should be established and followed, including rules for:

        - materials check-in and check-out;

        - password access to electronic files; and

- item review meetings, standard setting activities, and other instances where access to operational items is necessary.

8.1.3   To the extent that the primary service provider uses third parties, the primary service provider should adopt a comprehensive security plan that covers maintenance of security at subcontracted or vended sites. This plan should include the following:

- training and sharing training materials;

- rules for securing materials during the transfer between a third party and the service provider and the transfer between a third party and the client;

- rules for the disposal of secure materials at vended sites;

- security at the third party's site, such as a locked room to which access is limited; and

- nondisclosure agreements.

8.1.4   Internet connectivity should be limited to an as-needed basis, with required use of logs to monitor such access, and should not be available on machines that can access other sensitive/secure information.

8.1.5   A method for the secure electronic transfer of information should be established. Available methodologies may include:

- encrypted data exchange; and

- secure FTP sites.

8.1.6   Procedures to make and keep facilities secure should be established. These procedures should include the use of:

- identification badges;

- visitor policy regulations; and

- security systems, levels of access, and procedures for online security.

8.1.7 A plan should be developed to guide the item release process, as well as other legislated or legal aspects of the client requirements that might conflict with security procedures.

8.1.8 Periodic audits of security plans should be undertaken, documented, and reported by the service provider.

8.2 Training materials regarding security should be developed and training conducted, on topics including the use of appropriate agreements protecting intellectual property.

8.2.1 Procedures for training the service provider staff and subcontractors in security and the importance of security should be documented and implemented.

8.2.2 Nondisclosure agreements, confidentiality agreements, and employee verification and validation rules should be established and documented at every point where different service provider individuals have access to secure materials.

8.3 Policies and procedures for dealing with possible security breaches should be developed and implemented.

8.3.1 Procedures should be in place to prevent potential breaches in security. A plan should be developed that includes a recovery plan for any security breach and any potential consequences to individual(s) responsible for the breach. Plans should include procedures to be evoked if security breaches occur that jeopardize the integrity of student test score results. This breach protocol may include use of a breach test form.

8.3.2 Development of a breach test form should be coordinated with all program needs and requirements.

8.3.3 A communications plan should be developed to ensure that all stakeholders in the assessment are informed about the steps that should be taken if a breach occurs.

8.4 Procedures for test administration including the management of possible testing irregularities should be developed and implemented including attention to communicating those procedures to all necessary parties.

8.4.1　Secure administration procedures should be established and clearly communicated to the appropriate individuals. These procedures should ensure that the following items take place:

- proper handling of secure materials;

- secure storage of materials prior to, during, and after administration as delineated elsewhere in this chapter (see 8.5);

- proper handling of tests given with accommodations and/or in alternative assessment formats (e.g., testing in separate rooms, across multiple days, or using allowable accommodations); and

- signed confidentiality agreements/oaths are obtained from proctors and any others who have access to secure materials.

8.4.2　Rules and procedures to prevent and/or respond to instances of test administration irregularities and cheating should be developed and promulgated. These procedures may cover provisions for the following:

- training;

- proctor monitoring;

- seating charts; and

- explanation of consequences of testing irregularities and cheating.

8.5 Procedures should be developed and implemented to account for and protect secure materials at all stages of distribution, receipt, storage, and return.

8.5.1　These procedures should address how security issues will be managed at state and local levels.

8.5.2　The service provider and the client must ensure that secure materials are accounted for at all levels of distribution. This means that a documented chain of custody procedure should be established and put in place for tracking all secure assessment materials. Possible characteristics of such a system include:

- unique student ID numbers;
- unique document ID numbers;
- bar code labels;
- unique security ID numbers; and
- communication, explanation, and training for district/school staff.

8.5.3   Each document distributed should have a known and documented destination for distribution. Receipt procedures should be established and documented. These procedures should deal with the following:

- reconciling the expected quantity to be received with the actual quantity of documents received;
- maintaining documentation of returned and received materials;
- secure, traceable return methods; and
- developing a processing reconciliation procedure (to include a final accounting of materials), which may involve counting materials received as well as scanning receipts.

8.5.4   A plan to account for and obtain the return of all secure materials should be written. This plan should be clearly communicated to the appropriate individuals. It must be implemented by the appropriate staff. Any consequences associated with missing materials should be documented as part of the plan.

8.5.5   A plan for secure materials disposition and salvage should be established. This should be approved by the client. Components of this plan should include:

- a process for authorizing appropriate individuals to destroy materials;

- a process for proper handling of contaminated materials; and

- certification that materials were destroyed.

CHAPTER 9. TEST ADMINISTRATION

Introduction

This chapter highlights the best practices for administration of the assessments, which is critical to the inferences made from assessment results. The client and the service provider should collaborate to establish the most efficient test administration practices feasible while maintaining the standardization necessary across the state. After each administration, lessons learned should be reviewed and refinements, with appropriate planning, can be integrated into the next administration cycle.

9.1   **An annual calendar of assessments should be identified and published well in advance, which may be done for multiple years at one time, when practical.**

    9.1.1   The testing calendar should be available on the client's website and publicly announced at the time of posting.

    9.1.2   The final, approved testing calendar should not be altered or revised unless conditions make it absolutely necessary.

    9.1.3   If calendar changes are necessary, they should be negotiated with the service provider, announced, and version control implemented.

9.2   **The testing schedule should articulate which days each assessment will be administered and how much time will be devoted to each assessment. In addition, modifications in the testing schedule or in test administration procedures will be made for test takers needing more time, accommodations, and untimed assessments, where applicable (see Chapter 19).**

    9.2.1   A timing study should be conducted to validate the time needed to administer a new test.

    9.2.2   Time necessary for administration should include the following activities, as appropriate:

        • test administrator preparation prior to student engagement;

- student engagement of the test including sample items;

- test administrator close-out of administration session(s);

- use of multiple test segments during a single administration session;

- use of appropriate accommodations under the conditions documented in Chapter 19; and

- student breaks.

9.3 Coordination of statewide assessments requires specific roles to be defined at the state, district, and school levels.

9.3.1 Districts should designate a district assessment coordinator for all communications and coordination of state assessments.

9.3.2 Schools should designate a building assessment coordinator for all communications and coordination of state assessments.

9.3.3 Contact lists with email addresses should be maintained and used. These lists should include state, district, and building contacts.

9.4 To accommodate preparation needs, the service provider and client should agree on how and when student-level directions for administration should be made available prior to the administration window.

9.4.1 The client and service provider should agree upon how much time is sufficient prior to administration for delivery of materials. When directions contain secure material (i.e., assessment items), different delivery dates or special packing may be necessary.

9.4.2 Maintenance of security of such materials must be documented.

9.4.3 Non-secure manuals and directions should be posted to a website.

9.5 The protocol for preparing the testing environment will be outlined as a part of the procedure manuals and training.

9.5.1   The test administrator-to-student ratio should be identified, either as a requirement or recommendation.

9.5.2   Rooms for administration and their requirements, including allowable accommodations, should be identified. For example, allowable seating arrangements for administration need to be made.

9.5.3   Allowable and expressly prohibited materials for student use during administration should be identified (e.g., scratch paper and calculator are allowed, but PDAs are not).

9.5.4   Roles, responsibilities, and requirements for assessment proctors should be defined and implemented. For example, it should be obvious that parents cannot proctor their own children.

9.6   The service provider and the client will decide when and what materials and procedures, required for training and for administration of the assessment, will be made available in advance of the administration window.

9.6.1   Such materials and procedures may include training workshops and/or web-based components.

9.6.2   The client and the service provider should agree upon the nature and focus of audiences for the test coordinator material.

- Many states publish a manual of general procedures, for wide audiences, that provides guidance on topics such as the following:

    – an overview of the assessment program in the state, including state laws and regulations;

    – ethical practices for test administration;

    – roles and responsibilities of district and school staff during testing process;

    – a process for determining accommodations for qualifying students and a process for challenging these determinations;

- participation requirements for students in the assessment program, including those in unique circumstances (e.g., hospitalized students);

- general administration guidance, such as scheduling and documentation;

- provision of an accurate student information and demographics;

- reports available following the administration;

- necessary forms used within the assessment program; and

- information on policies for score appeals, school security breaches, test irregularities, or public review of assessments.

- Many states publish administration manuals that are specific to a particular assessment, and are geared to district and school administrator use during the time of an administration. These manuals may include the following information:

- general information about particular assessments, including websites and customer service contacts;

- procedures for administering alternative assessment forms, and/or alternate assessments, to special populations, including information on the state accommodation policy and allowable accommodations for all forms and alternate assessments;

- procedures for ordering additional materials;

- preparation of testing sites;

- secure distribution of test materials;

- maintaining a secure inventory of returned test materials;

- procedures for returning test materials to the service provider; and

- forms used during the administration.

9.6.3 Training protocol for test administrators should be standardized across the state. Training protocol and materials should specify:

- the length of training;

- the agenda for and objectives of training; and

- the procedures for conducting training with test administrators.

9.6.4 At the end of training, test administrators should be familiar with, at a minimum:

- the administration plan for the assessment (e.g., multiple segments on particular days);

- procedures for administering the assessment under normal standardized conditions;

- procedures for reporting and correcting flaws in the test materials;

- procedures for reporting test administration irregularities and security breaches;

- procedures for dealing with cases involving suspected student collusion;

- assessment procedures when unique circumstances arise (e.g., fire alarms, power failures, severe weather alerts, student illness during administration);

- protocol for answering student questions about the assessment;

- procedures for handling allowable accommodations for any assessment, including any alternative assessment forms, or for the use of alternate assessments consistent with the practices described in Chapter 19;

- procedures for ensuring test security during all stages of administration, including on-site storage, pursuant to the practices set forth in Chapter 8; and

- procedures for allowable student activities after completing the assessment if other students are still engaged in the assessment.

9.7   Student-level directions for an administration must specify the exact language to be recited to the students.

9.7.1   Scripted directions for students must make clear what is to be spoken aloud by the test administrator and what the procedural directions should be for the test administrator.

9.7.2   Scripted directions for students should be written specifically for each grade level and content assessment.

9.7.3   Scripted directions for students should include instructions and/or provisions for different administration configurations for the assessment (e.g., multiple segments on a single day; individual segments on separate days).

9.7.4   Individuals who are not familiar with the program should review scripted student directions. This will help to ensure clarity and accuracy. For example, individuals could play the roles of administrators, teachers/proctors, and students to resolve any discrepancies.

CHAPTER 10. MATERIALS PACKAGING

Introduction

Best practices for packaging all client materials, including secure and ancillary materials, require systems and procedures designed to ensure accuracy in both order creation and fulfillment. The ability to expedite these processes is also requisite, as well as the creation of accessible documentation to assist in problem resolution.

For this phase of the overall development process, it is essential that materials be organized in the most intuitive manner possible, and adequate documentation be provided, in order to facilitate efficient and accurate receipt and tracking of all materials.

10.1 A process will be established to ensure the accurate and timely packaging of orders, including additional material orders.

    10.1.1 A process should be established to create packing lists based upon supplied requirements. Material types may include any accommodated versions, quantities, and material destinations. The process should be documented and agreed upon by the client and service provider.

    10.1.2 A procedure to help ensure that the proper assembly of materials is specifically assigned to a destination should be established, and may include use of:

- bar codes;

- checklists; and

- lot sampling.

    10.1.3 A process to reconcile original orders and any additional orders should be established.

10.2 A process should be established to ensure the accurate labeling of all completed packages.

    10.2.1 This procedure should include information regarding how box sequencing (e.g., Box 1 of N) and the total number of boxes will be displayed. Labels should:

- contain up-to-date address and contact information; and

- be placed on boxes according to specifications agreed upon by the client and service provider.

10.3 Expedited packaging and shipping requirements should be developed and agreed upon by the client and service provider.

10.4 A plan should be developed for packaging and shipping of the breach form, if necessary.

10.5 A process should be established to ensure documentation is created and maintained for all completed orders.

10.5.1 A procedure should be created to help ensure access to documentation, including security checklists and packing lists, for the service provider's management personnel to respond to client inquiries.

10.5.2 A packing list for each box, as well as a report or schematic describing layout of materials included, should be available to the individual receiving the shipment.

CHAPTER 11. TRANSPORTATION OF MATERIALS AND CHAIN OF CUSTODY MANAGEMENT

Introduction

At different times in the assessment life cycle, materials need to be transported and managed between different service providers, schools, and students. The most prevalent example is the production of test materials (test books, answer documents, coordinator manuals, and other ancillaries) by different service providers and subcontractors. These materials must be brought together to be assembled into packages and shipped. Transportation staff handles the movement of materials between sites. Due to the highly-sensitive nature of the materials, a chain of custody must be maintained at every step to ensure the security and integrity of the assessment content. The management of this chain of custody should be apparent in and between all steps of the materials handling process (e.g., production, printing, packaging, distribution, and retrieval of test materials). It also should be apparent in the printing and distribution of reports. It is imperative that all hand-offs are managed appropriately between affected stakeholders, including service provider, subcontractors, and departments of education, districts, school officials, and test takers.

This chapter describes best practices for the transportation and hand-off of materials between key stakeholders and reinforces the management of the materials through the chain of custody. Generally, it covers practices to be referenced when materials are transported from one stakeholder to another.

11.1 **All changes in the custody of materials will be identified in advance of program implementation. A change in custody occurs when different stakeholders are responsible for separate tasks/activities that occur along the assessment lifecycle. Each task is owned by a stakeholder, and as such each stakeholder is responsible to be a sender and/or receiver of materials.**

11.1.1 Stakeholders responsible for sending or receiving materials might include the service provider, subcontractors, state, district, or school officials, and test takers.

11.1.2 Changes in custody may also occur between different processes, such as content production, materials printing (including proofs), packaging and assembly, distribution to districts and schools, distribution within schools and classrooms, delivery to the scoring service provider (return instructions provided), delivery to the security service provider (return instructions provided), and production and assembly of paper reports.

11.2 The service provider will ensure the security, integrity, and accuracy of materials shipped, transported, and received while maintaining this chain of custody.

11.2.1 These definitions describe the links in the chain of custody:

- **Shipper**: any stakeholder sending materials to another stakeholder;

- **Transporter**: any transportation provider; and

- **Receiver**: any stakeholder receiving materials from another stakeholder.

11.2.1 All stakeholder facilities must be secure. This might include the use of security guards and restricted areas based on employee type. Security is discussed in more detail in Chapter 8.

11.2.2 Test materials must also be protected from damage that may affect their use, such as exposure to the weather, direct sunlight and other variances in atmosphere.

11.2.3 Shipper responsibilities might include:

- ensuring accurate quantities are shipped;

- using packing slips reflecting correct quantities;

- using a bill of lading for freight shipments;

- ensuring accurate information on shipping labels;

- ensuring shipping labels are identifiable on each package;

- using pallet maps;

- using security checklists;

- obtaining all required signatures on shipped packages; and

- providing electronic tracking of shipments.

11.2.4 Transporter responsibilities may include:

- ensuring packages accepted match the bill of lading;

- reviewing credentials or permissions allowing transportation;

- using appropriate vehicles for security and to protect packages;

- accommodating dock restrictions of the shipper and receiver;

- providing traceability of packages; and

- obtaining all required signatures.

11.2.5 Receiver responsibilities may include:

- checking the physical condition of materials;

- following procedures and protocols established by the service provider if materials are damaged; and

- ensuring accepted packages match bill of lading.

11.3 State, District, and School officials will establish a chain of custody for hand-offs to ensure that documents are received, accounted for, distributed and returned.

11.3.1 Test Coordinators should account for materials received from the service provider, including conducting the following steps:

- comparing and verifying that the materials are organized by teacher or grade group using the packing slip;

- making use of the security checklist (when contracted) to verify materials; and

- reporting any missing materials according to established procedures.

11.3.2 Protocols should be developed to deal with the hand-off of materials among test coordinators and test administrators to ensure the materials get to the correct test takers.

11.3.3 When additional materials are needed, the processes should be established to request materials with school or district officials.

11.3.4 Scorable and secure materials should be reassembled according to the instructions provided by the service provider.

11.3.5 Materials should be shipped to the service provider according to the instructions provided by the service provider.

11.3.6 The client and the service provider should jointly establish procedures for recovering materials, including administered tests, from tardy districts and schools.

CHAPTER 12. RECEIVING, CHECK-IN, AND PROCESSING OF MATERIALS

Introduction

When materials are received at a scoring site they must be prepared for processing. Scorable materials should be sorted and compiled to ensure that tests are grouped correctly prior to scanning. This preparation often includes accounting for each district and ensuring that the tests are aligned correctly under the appropriate header sheets. It is important to scan tests within the correct hierarchy to ensure accurate data management and aggregate/disaggregate reporting.

Secure materials should be sorted and grouped, which usually occurs at several levels, such as by class or grade within a school and by school within a district. This allows for correct accounting and reconciliation for each group once security reports are produced.

12.1 A process will be established to ensure accurate receipt, check-in, and processing of materials at the processing center.

12.1.1 Receipt by all districts and schools should be verified using a checklist.

12.1.2 Receipt of all packages by the district should be verified against the total number of packages shipped.

12.1.3 Scorable and secure non-scorable materials arriving at the same location should be entered into separate workflows.

12.1.4 Scorable materials should be checked into workflow to be tracked through processing.

12.1.5 Processing rules and specifications should be established.

12.1.6 Processes should be established with customers to communicate and resolve issues.

12.1.7 Training protocols for material handlers should be established.

12.1.8   Documents should be removed from packages by trained handlers.

12.1.9   Documents should be sorted by building and teacher/grade group.

12.1.10 Documents should be aligned based on orientation and location of identifying marks.

12.1.11 Extraneous materials should be removed.

12.1.12 Document counts should be verified.

12.1.13 Documents should be assembled to ensure correct hierarchical integrity.

12.1.14 Processing rules to ensure that buildings are shown within the correct district should be established.

12.1.15 Processing rules to ensure that teacher/grade groups exist within the correct building should be established.

12.1.16 Documents should be stacked or bundled to ensure hierarchy integrity and to provide the ability to rebuild the stacks if documents come out of order.

12.2 A process will be established to reconcile and report any missing packages or material.

CHAPTER 13. SCANNING AND POST-SCANNING EDITING

Introduction

Best practices in this chapter describe the processes and procedures that are necessary to ensure accuracy throughout the scanning and editing of student answer documents. Generally, it is the responsibility of:

- the service provider to provide an environment that achieves the highest possible degree of accuracy throughout this critical phase; and
- the client, in concert with the service provider, to develop detailed specifications for the editing rules to be applied to student demographic and item response information.

13.1 A process should be established to ensure accurate scanning.

13.1.1 Documents to be scanned should meet production specifications as defined by relevant technologies. For example, specifications should include rules and procedures for the use of:

- anchor points;

- timing tracks; and

- dropout ink.

13.1.2 Documents should be scanned in a secure, climate-controlled environment. If necessary, documents should be conditioned/acclimatized prior to scanning.

13.1.3 The scanning hardware and supporting software should be calibrated and the calibration procedures should be documented.

13.1.4 Scanner operators should be trained and training should be documented.

13.1.5 A specifications document should be created and agreed upon by the client and the service provider that delineates the attributes of the scoring process (i.e., how a mark is recognized and scored). These attributes should include:

- multiple marks;

- incomplete marks;

- light marks;

- erasures; and

- other nonconforming marks.

13.1.6 Processes should be established and used to verify the accuracy of the scanning hardware and supporting software. These processes should include use of:

- a test deck or other appropriate process to demonstrate the accuracy of data collected on each scanner;

- a User Acceptance Test (UAT); and

- an established hardware maintenance protocol.

13.1.7 When a scanner fails to meet calibration requirements, there should be a plan to intervene and to identify documents and data potentially affected. A plan to rescan affected documents, if required, should be developed and implemented.

13.2 A process should be established to ensure that booklet integrity and student response document integrity are maintained during the scanning process (i.e., the correct pages are scanned, in order, and the page counts match the booklet specifications).

13.2.1 The documents should be checked for total page count.

13.2.2 The documents should be checked for image completeness and clarity.

13.2.3 A litho code, bar code, or other identifying strategy should be used on each page or sheet.

13.3 A process should be established to ensure that all documents requiring scanning are scanned.

13.3.1 An exception-handling process for damaged and unscannable documents should be developed and documented. This process should include:

- key entry with verification;

- flatbed image scanning; and

- alternative processing, if applicable.

13.3.2   A procedure should be in place to reconcile the number of scannable documents received with the number of documents actually scanned.

13.4 An editing process should be established to ensure accurate collection of data from scanned documents.

13.4.1   A specification document should be created that delineates how a mark read by the scanner is identified and edited. This document should cover the following issues:

- identification of appropriate values for all edited fields (e.g., names as A-Z, multiple choice options as 1-4, etc.);

- multiple marks;

- omitted marks (i.e., leading, trailing, or embedded);

- blanks; and

- editing quality control rules.

13.4.2   A User Acceptance Test (UAT) of the editing software should be completed prior to implementation of the full production system.

13.4.3   Editors should be trained and training should be documented.

13.5 A contingency plan or system, approved by both the service provider and the client, should be developed and implemented so that any issues encountered in scanning will not delay scoring and reporting.

CHAPTER 14. SCORING OPEN-ENDED RESPONSES

Introduction

Scoring quality of open-ended responses remains an important component of a high quality assessment program. Scores assigned to students that respond to open-ended questions must be reliable to ensure an accurate reflection of student performance on these items. There are several factors that impact the quality of rating open-ended responses, including rater training processes, rater staffing processes, and quality assurance processes. Also, appropriate consideration should be given to associated elements of open-response scoring, such as security and confidentiality of student information. The practices below address these and other considerations of open-ended scoring.

14.1 Processes should be established to ensure the accuracy and reliability of open-ended scoring.

14.1.1 Student handwritten responses to open-ended questions should be scored by trained and qualified human raters.

14.1.2 The plan for rater training and for rater qualifying to score should be documented and approved by the client.

14.1.3 General rater hiring standards should be documented and available to the client.

14.1.4 Rater training and the process of rater qualifying to score should be based on input from subject-matter experts in the area being scored and approved by the client.

14.1.5 Rater qualification statistics should be collected and documented.

14.1.6 Training materials used for rater training or qualification should represent student responses across the entire population of possible student response submissions. Materials should include a range of score points, types and styles of writing, information on disregarding cues related to disability or accommodations that are unrelated to scoring criteria, and other relevant considerations.

14.1.7 Materials used during rater training may include rangefinders, anchor papers and other scoring materials, including training or qualification papers. Materials should go through an agreed-upon approval process before use in training.

14.1.8 Field-test scoring of open-ended responses should mimic operational scoring, to the extent possible, and ensure the use of:

- similar rater selection protocols; and

- similar training and qualification standards.

14.1.9 If artificial intelligence scoring procedures are used, these procedures should meet the same standards for accuracy and reliability that exist for human scoring of the same item type. Methods for training the artificial intelligence scoring engines and evidence that the engine meets accuracy and reliability standards should be documented.

14.2 Processes should be established to ensure consistent hand-scoring results of open-ended responses. These results should meet predefined target expectations and specifications agreed upon by the client and the service provider.

14.2.1 Quality checks should be conducted throughout the scoring process.

14.2.2 Individual and group rater performance should be measured and analyzed regularly.

14.2.3 When performance of an individual rater and/or a group of raters falls outside of target expectations, corrective action should be taken. This may include retraining of raters and re-scoring of selected student responses. The process for making a decision to retrain raters, and/or re-score selected student responses, should be established ahead of time and should be driven by score quality considerations, and should be agreed upon by the client and service provider.

14.2.4 Validity papers or check-sets, consisting of previously scored student responses, may be administered to check on rater accuracy.

14.2.5   Scores assigned by raters to selected student responses should be confirmed with scores from other expert raters as a mechanism to monitor rater accuracy.

14.2.6   If artificial intelligence procedures are used, the client and the service provider should agree on usage (initial read or reread score).

14.2.7   Inter-rater reliability data should be collected by sampling a percentage of papers for additional ratings. These additional ratings may be performed by other qualified raters, expert raters, or by the computer making use of artificial intelligence procedures. If the contract requires resolution when there is non-perfect agreement of rater scores, a procedure for resolving score discrepancies (sometimes called adjudication) should be developed, agreed upon by the client and the service provider, documented, and followed during scoring.

14.2.8   Any measure or analysis used to check accuracy and reliability of the hand-scoring process should be made available for the client's review.

14.2.9   A plan for the machine scoring of any multiple choice items included with the open-ended response items should be developed and approved by the service provider and the client. As part of this plan:

- the programming of the answer key should be checked by staff, independent of programmers; and

- a test deck should be used to check the accuracy of scoring.

14.3 A procedure should be established to identify, evaluate, and if necessary escalate to the client, student responses that contain disturbing content.

14.3.1   This escalation process to the client or the client's representative should promptly follow discovery of any disturbing content and should include confirmation of disturbing content by rating leaders, scoring directors, or other service provider scoring officials.

14.3.2 The client and the service provider should establish and agree upon rules that guide the scoring service provider in identifying disturbing content.

14.3.3 Rules about reporting disturbing student responses to appropriate governing authorities of the client should be developed and followed by the service provider and the client.

14.4 A plan should be developed and agreed upon by the service provider and the client that delineates the process for re-scoring, late batch scoring, and score verification requests.

14.5 A process should be defined and approved by the client and the service provider to resolve requests for re-scoring of hand-scored open-ended responses. This process should contain:

- a schedule for re-scoring based on score verification requests;
- a method for logging results from re-scoring;
- a method for communicating re-scoring results; and
- a method for updating data sets and score reports and informing other users of updated results.

14.6 The procedures established for the scoring process should ensure that confidentiality is maintained and student identity is securely controlled.

14.6.1 Raters should only see the student response and no other identifying information related to the student.

14.6.2 Standard security procedures, as defined elsewhere in this document, should be followed during hand-scoring as well as during other processing.

14.7 Processes should be established to perform hand-scoring verifications of machine-scored items that are included on the test.

14.7.1 Standards should be available to use as part of a mark interpretation guide.

14.7.2 A training program should be in place to qualify individuals.

14.7.3 Original documents should be used for verification.

14.7.4 All discrepancies should be tracked, investigated, and documented.

14.7.5 Performance metrics should be collected to determine the rate of disagreement.

14.7.6 A plan for corrective action should be developed, if needed.

14.7.7 The agreed upon corrective action plan should be used when defects are discovered, such as the use of root cause analysis and defects tracking tools.

14.7.8 Student data resulting from scoring shall be considered secure information (see Chapter 8).

14.7.9 The service provider should provide for hand-scoring of the breach form, if it is within contract scope.

14.7.10 Storage and retention of original and hand-scored student work should follow the plan established and agreed upon by the service provider and the client.

CHAPTER 15. ONLINE ASSESSMENT AND TECHNICAL SUPPORT

Introduction

This chapter describes operational best practices for computer-based testing (CBT). While the evolution of CBT has continued since its inception in the late 1970s, its proliferation into large-scale assessment is still relatively new. As such, many of the procedures and processes outlined below are more aspirational in nature or simply represent current practices as opposed to defined state-of-the-art practices. As the use of online testing expands, additional best practices are likely to emerge.

15.1 **Requirements for the use of any software, for or by either the client or the service provider, should be clearly documented and explained, including the use of supporting devices such as printers, scanners, or other information collection or display devices. These requirements will be made available in a user's manual or other document. Such requirements and specifications should include the following:**

- a description of the platforms and environment required to support software including:

    - requirements for PC-compatible computer environments; and

    - requirements for Macintosh-compatible computer environments;

- complete instructions for downloading and installation of software, drivers, or other required components should be included, as well as instructions for removal. Ideally, this would include troubleshooting guides and installation support opportunities, if applicable;

- a procedure, such as a "wizard," to allow for testing of the accuracy of the software, or the proper installation and functioning of other components prior to testing;

- procedures for the end user, including specific instructions in the event of a service interruption due to software, internet, or LAN malfunction; and

- requirements of the assessment software regarding the use of technology with internet connections, local networks, or local configurations, including the following technological elements:

  – firewalls;

  – antivirus software;

  – network security applications;

  – pop-up blockers;

  – anti-spam applications;

  – e-mail filters;

  – applications running in background; and

  – schedulers.

15.2 The minimum and preferred technology infrastructure needed to support online testing should be documented and explained. Preferably, such requirements should be provided via a technology wizard or application that could be executed in the local environment to mimic conditions anticipated during live testing. Minimum requirements should support the verification of infrastructure readiness either by using a checklist or automated application.

15.3 The technical support documents should include information about suggested computer lab configurations. Many school computer labs are set up to support instruction and not assessment. These labs may need to be reconfigured. Online assessment proctors should be informed about how to reconfigure the labs, how long the reconfiguration will take, and any additional precautions (such as vision blockers) that should be taken prior to testing.

15.4 Information on computer-based assistive technologies should be provided to the client so that the client can evaluate which, if any, computer assistive technologies it will allow. Data on the use of these technologies should be collected.

15.5 A practice test should be provided to allow students to become familiar with keyboarding and navigation techniques and tools that will be used during the live assessment. Some clients will want to create a training environment that allows students to explore an on-demand practice module.

15.6 Procedures for students to enroll in the online assessment system should be provided, as well as instructions and procedures for modification of enrollment data, where permitted by the client, including the following:

- correcting or modifying demographic data;

- adding new test takers;

- applying or modifying codes and classifications for special conditions such as absenteeism, disability category, and use of accommodations; and

- modifying other student information and/or conditions.

15.7 Information on the availability of results, their format, and when they will be made available following the online assessment should be provided. This information should clearly differentiate between operational and field test data and information.

15.8 Procedures for maintaining the security of the online testing environment should be documented. These procedures may include the following:

- locking down the computer desktop;

- securing cell phones, memory sticks, or other media collection devices prior to testing;

- identifying students by using a testing roster;

- adhering to standard administration security procedures, as described elsewhere in this document; and

- establishing security codes for adding, editing, or removing authorized users of the system.

15.9 A description of the roles of test administrator, computer lab coordinator, and test proctor for online assessment should be developed and implemented.

15.10 Specific training procedures for each role should be established and the training should be documented. These procedures should include but not be limited to:

- contact information for technical help;

- descriptions of the roles and responsibilities for all parties that will address questions, logistical problems and technical errors during the test;

- processes for answering content knowledge questions, and by whom;

- processes for resolving technical questions or issues during the test;

- processes for determining who will answer questions regarding the technical or online application versus issues concerning application disruption;

- processes for responding to local network conflicts or internet provider issues with connectivity;

- description of the expected duration for responses and wait times; and

- description of the location of user guides, FAQs, other resource documents, and the process that will be used to keep them updated for continued accuracy.

15.11 Technical support should be available via telephone and/ or electronically with tools such as a help desk and/or e-mail account. These services should be managed by persons with knowledge of the online system, procedures, and tools.

15.12 Metrics for systems performance should be identified. This may include but is not limited to:

- latency, hours of operation;

- planned hours for service; and

- system interruptions.

CHAPTER 16.TECHNICAL DEFENSIBILITY

Introduction

The extent to which assessment results are appropriate for their intended use is largely dependent on the implementation of procedures that are consistent with industry standards for technical defensibility. Although these *Best Practices* are not themselves surrogates for the *Standards for Educational and Psychological Testing*, they are intended to be consistent with those professional and technical standards by addressing the operational aspects related to a statewide assessment program. Such procedures or practices help ensure that the inferences derived from the assessment results are reliable and valid.

16.1   **Procedures should be established and implemented to ensure that the assessment is consistent with industry standards for technical defensibility.**

16.1.1   Established standards addressing technical and professional aspects of assessment development should be followed, especially the AERA, APA, and NCME *Standards for Educational and Psychological Testing*.

16.1.2   The assessment should adhere to relevant regulations and guidance documents, especially standards provided by the United States Department of Education for accountability assessments of general education, special education, and English language development programs. This should include peer review standards and updates, revisions, or replacements of such technical guidance provided by the US Department of Education.

16.1.3   The client is responsible for articulating the intended uses of the assessment and for identifying the authorization for the assessment.

16.1.4   The client and the service provider should jointly review and agree on key technical deliverables, these may include:

• item and form blueprints and specifications;

• procedures and analyses to detect possible bias;

- rubrics and keys to be used for scoring, including instructions for scoring assessments where accommodations have been allowed;

- field-test sampling plans;

- parameter estimates for all field tested items;

- alignment studies;

- comparability studies, as needed, for changes to assessments;

- specification of the measurement model and analyses of model fit;

- parameter estimates and other item statistics for operational items;

- standard setting procedures and results;

- equating plan, procedures, and results;

- score-to-scale conversion rules and tables;

- development of vertical scales;

- stability of sub-scale scores that may be reported in addition to the total scores;

- analyses of conditional and total-test reliability as well as classification accuracy and consistency;

- analyses and research conducted to establish the validity of inferences drawn from the assessment results;

- disaggregation of data by predefined groups;

- score report designs and descriptions of performance levels;

- data analyses to check on potential security breaches; and

- erasure analysis and other statistical procedures to detect response integrity.

16.1.5   The service provider should produce technical reports that document results of creation and use of technical deliverables.

16.1.6   The contents of any technical reports should be jointly agreed upon in advance of preparation by the client and the service provider.

16.1.7   The frequency and timeline for production of all reports should be jointly established by the client and the service provider.

16.1.8   The client is responsible for final approval of technical reports and arranging any appropriate access to such materials.

16.1.9   An independent Technical Advisory Committee (TAC), composed of members with familiarity in measuring all student populations, should review and endorse the procedures used in development, scoring, analysis, and reporting.

CHAPTER 17. SCORE REPORTING

Introduction

Score reports are the most visible yet most misunderstood products of any assessment. Score reports often are used in isolation and should, to the extent possible, be able to "stand on their own." Thus, score reports and associated interpretive information should receive the same level of attention to detail and thoughtfulness as that required for test design. This chapter is aimed at ensuring the high technical quality of reports and their linkage to assessment program data, regardless of the types of assessments used.

This chapter also covers best practices regarding the purpose and audience for reports, as well as steps for ensuring that reports are readily accessible. For most assessment programs, report interpretation guides are written for specific audiences (i.e., parents, teachers, and school/district administration staff). The intent of these guides is to provide explanations of the reports that use "non-technical language" to explain how the results in the reports might be interpreted.

Finally, this chapter deals with best practices covering the distribution of reports and associated guides, both in paper and electronic formats.

17.1 A process should be developed to design and approve program-specific operational score reports that are required for the assessment program, students, classes, schools, and districts.

    17.1.1   The process should include definitions and specifications for each report, including purpose, audience, level of aggregation and/or disaggregation by student subgroups, business rules for all data elements and calculations, performance level and strand/standard information, physical design, and delivery mode.

17.1.2   A shell or mock-up of every report populated with simulated data should be created for review and publication. When feasible, those mock-ups should be shared with all user groups to ascertain if there are problems with understanding the reports or their accessibility.

17.1.3   Report-specific decision rules that define the inclusion specifications and calculations associated with each data element cell should be developed and agreed upon by the client and service provider.

17.1.4   The client should identify to the service provider any relevant state and federal laws pertaining to confidentiality and the reporting of sensitive data. Pertinent laws should be addressed with specific reporting specifications.

17.2   Prior to reporting, the service provider and the client should review a representative sample of actual reports, data files, and related materials as a quality control check of design and decision rules.

17.2.1   The client and the service provider should agree on a sample and independently verify that all requirements are met.

17.2.2   The client and the service provider should document the approval of each report, whether by signature, electronic means, or otherwise.

17.3   Specifications for interpretative guides for relevant reports, including style guidelines and content outlines, should be defined.

17.3.1   The client should identify reports requiring interpretation guides.

17.3.2   The client and the service provider should develop a set of stylistic guidelines for development of each guide, including layout specifications.

17.3.3   All numerical reports used in an interpretive guide should be populated with simulated and reasonably representative data.

17.3.4   The service provider should develop each required interpretative guide for review and approval by the client.

17.4   The distribution strategy should be defined by the client and the service provider for each reporting cycle.

17.4.1   For paper-based materials (reports and interpretive guides), the service provider and the client should develop an approved specification for the number of copies, order of reports, distribution, and packaging.

17.4.2   For secure web-based posting of reports, the service provider and the client should develop specifications for access and distribution, including security levels and access procedures.

CHAPTER 18. DATA MANAGEMENT

Introduction

There are many points within the assessment life cycle where secure data are stored, changed, transmitted, computed, analyzed, and reported. Data are of the utmost importance to an assessment program because they provide the means by which critical decisions can be made. Procedures and protocols should be developed and followed to maintain accuracy, security, and integrity of the data. This chapter addresses types of secure data as well as the management of secure data, including points of transfer between stakeholders, along with changes, archival, and disposition of the data.

18.1   **Data to be collected and managed should be defined and documented. Such data should include:**

- item data (e.g., content, key);

- enrollment data (e.g., district and school names, grade spans, addresses, student counts);

- score recipient data (e.g., score recipient preferences and institutional data such as mail to and bill to addresses);

- student demographics (e.g., student names, IDs, gender, DOB) should be included within a barcode file, on an answer document, or via an online interface;

- specific accommodations used on each assessment;

- student responses (e.g., multiple choice, images of constructed responses) from an answer document or via an online interface; and

- scores (e.g., student, aggregate, disaggregate) on paper reports, through electronic medium, or via an online interface.

18.2   **Rules should be defined for how to collect, verify, update, share, archive, and dispose of secure data.**

18.2.1 Rules should be established on how data can be transferred between stakeholders. Data are often shared between stakeholders, most often between the client and the service provider, but data are also transferred between district and school staff, where appropriate. Examples for how these data are shared include FTP sites, e-mail, and service provider supplied online interfaces. Typically, secure FTP sites and service provider online interfaces allow for secure transfer of data while regular FTP sites and e-mail do not.

18.2.2 In instances where the client possesses a Student Information System (SIS) to export data, rules should be constructed for how the resulting data file can be used as a source for student enrollment data. The following should be considered when developing the enrollment file:

- formats to receive and process files;

- procedures for validating information; and

- rules for the appropriate use of data.

18.2.3 File formats must be defined to ensure that data populate correctly during exports and imports across different databases. This formatting includes types of fields, number of fields, field lengths, alpha and/or numeric limitations, and descriptions of data elements. Processes should be established to verify formats by using test runs of mock data.

18.2.4 A file transmission service should allow for monitoring of transmissions (confirmation of successful delivery or successful FTP).

18.2.5 When data are presented online (testing and reporting), the use of IDs and passwords must be used to ensure correct level of data access.

18.2.6 Rules should be established on the timing and frequency for when data are collected and transferred, as well as the parties responsible for the verification, updating, and transfer of data. Special attention should be paid to data elements that may change from initial collection to actual use (e.g., school addresses, grade spans, and key contacts can all change "without warning").

18.2.7   The service provider should establish rules on how it uses and allows data access within its system.

18.2.8   Rules should be established for the length of time, format, and level that data should be archived.

18.2.9   Rules should be established for the disposition of data.

18.2.10   A data change process should be incorporated to allow the client to change data if and when it is reasonable and/or feasible to do so.

CHAPTER 19. ASSESSMENT OF SPECIAL POPULATIONS

Introduction

Although most statewide assessments are, by definition, standardized, they should be designed and administered in such a manner as to be fair and accessible for diverse groups of test-takers. In particular, care should be taken to ensure that students with disabilities and students who are English Language Learners (ELLs) have every reasonable opportunity to demonstrate what they know and can do on the assessment. This objective can be best accomplished by following established professional practices in item and test form design and by ensuring that the appropriate accommodations are offered pursuant to the written contract between the client and the service provider.

19.1   A process should be established and implemented to ensure that test items and forms are developed in accordance with the principles of universal design. As part of this process:

19.1.1   Items should be written to reduce construct irrelevance, to the extent possible (e.g., eliminate unnecessary reading load on mathematics items).

19.1.2   Items should be free of language or attributes that may offend or disadvantage test-takers from any subgroup.

19.1.3   Field tests should include students from special populations.

19.1.4   Empirical analyses should be conducted to provide information regarding how items are functioning for key subgroups.

19.1.5   Instructions should be written in clear language so that they are easy to understand by all test-takers. When possible, sample items or tasks should be provided.

19.1.6   Items should be reviewed by staff with expertise or experience with test-takers from special populations.

19.1.7 Specifications should be developed and implemented to ensure that items and forms are designed to be clear and legible. Such specifications may address the following:

- organization and sequencing of items;

- presentation of response options;

- positioning of items and passages, and/or other stimuli;

- type size and typeface;

- margins and blank space;

- clarity of graphics and/or item stimuli; and

- rules for emphasizing words or phrases (e.g. bold, capital letters, or underline).

19.2 Appropriate allowable accommodations, as called for in the written contract between the client and the service provider, shall be offered for test-takers with disabilities or test-takers who are English Language Learners (ELLs), where feasible and appropriate.

19.2.1 A list of allowable accommodations should be developed and specified by the service provider under the terms of the contract and be based on currently available evidence, including information obtained by reviewing relevant Individual Education Plans (IEPs) and 504 plans.

19.2.2 Allowable accommodations should be offered to students with disabilities based on the list developed by the service provider in conjunction with the individual student's IEP or 504 plan.

19.2.3 Large print and Braille test versions should be available for students who are visually impaired.

19.2.4 Signed versions should be available for students who are deaf or hard of hearing.

19.2.5 Supplemental materials such as adaptive rulers should be provided, when appropriate, for the subject matter being tested.

19.2.6   Tests to be delivered in languages other than English should be provided, as appropriate.

19.2.7   Assistative technology and/or procedures for oral reading should be available from the client for students that qualify.

19.2.8   The impact of accommodations, if any, on assessment results should be explained to test-takers.

19.2.9   Accommodations should be consistent to the extent possible for different modes of test administration or presentation (e.g., computer-based or paper-based testing).

19.3   **Where appropriate and necessary, the client and the service provider should agree on the development of alternate assessments.**

CHAPTER 20. ASSESSMENT PROGRAM PROCUREMENT

Introduction

The client procuring entity will write a solicitation document (e.g., an RFP, RFQ, RFS, ITB, etc., hereby referred to as an RFP) that contains sufficient information to allow all qualified bidders to understand the scope and specifications of the program being bid. Best practices for preparing and dealing with the procurement process are provided in this chapter.

20.1 **The client should provide a written overview of the program being bid, including the following:**

- a history of any related assessment programs that the entity has implemented;

- a description of the nature and purpose of the present proposed assessment program;

- the products and services being solicited;

- the beginning and ending dates of the proposed program;

- the proposal timeline with key procurement dates specified;

- the program timeline with major milestone dates within each school, calendar, or fiscal year that include administration dates of the assessments that the new contractor will be responsible for developing and/ or administering during each year;

- the mandatory requirements of a bidding company, including staffing, that must be met for the proposal to be judged as responsive to the RFP;

- a transition plan to describe services to be transferred at contract inception and contract closure (e.g., materials, data, etc.); and

- any special considerations unique to the client, such as specific procurement laws.

20.2 The client should provide a complete written description of how the proposal should be written, formatted, packaged, and delivered.

20.2.1   Sections of the RFP that are intended as background information or general descriptions should be distinguished from sections of the RFP that require responses from the bidder.

20.2.2   If the client intends to have sections of the RFP, to which a response is required, copied into proposal so that those copied sections precede each response—that format should be specified.

20.2.3   If the client requires key questions to be answered by the bidder, then those questions should be given in the RFP.

20.2.4   If page layout of the proposal (margins, line spacing, fonts and type sizes, page numbering, etc.) is important to the client, it should be specified.

20.2.5   Whether the proposal should be bound into single binder, or multiple binders, and whether these binders should be included in the same shipping boxes or packaged in different shipping boxes should be specified.

20.2.6   Delivery date and time, the person to whom the shipping boxes should be addressed, the address where boxes should be shipped, and any other instructions for identifying the boxes should be given in the RFP.

20.2.7   If electronic submission of the proposal is allowed or required, there should be detailed instructions and support for uploading all files.

20.3 The client should allow bidders to submit questions about the RFP. These questions should enable both RFP authors and bidders to clarify the meaning, intent, and requirements of the RFP.

20.3.1   Questions should be solicited early in the RFP process and responses to questions should be returned as rapidly as possible. Whether answers to questions will be provided to all bidders should be stated at the outset of the process.

20.3.2   Time should be built into the proposal process to allow for follow-up questions after the first round of questions and answers.

20.4   Specifications for a new assessment should be described as completely as possible.

20.4.1   Specifications for a new assessment should be compared and contrasted with those for the current assessment, when practical and feasible.

20.4.2   Specifications for a new assessment should include material on how universal design principles are to be implemented into the assessment development process.

20.4.3   If a proposed new assessment builds upon (i.e., is relevant to) one that currently exists, test specifications for the existing assessment should be available to all bidders within the RFP or by links to a website where the relevant documents exist.

20.4.4   All important specifications should be provided to prospective bidders, including:

- the test-taker N-counts;

- the N-counts of operational items per content area test, per grade;

- the number of forms per administration per year;

- the item types used within each test;

- examples of electronic item formats (e.g., XML) to evaluate item portability;

- requirements for stimulus-based items;

- how new items are field tested;

- psychometric approach to item calibration, scaling, and forms equating;

- design of test booklets and answer documents;

- security requirements for test materials;

- scoring requirements; and

- examples of individual and group score reports.

20.4.5　If the procuring entity wishes that the successful service provider suggest new or specific approaches for any part of the design or implementation of new assessment, this should be stated.

20.4.6　Item specifications, test specifications, a materials list and specifications, scoring specifications, reporting specifications, and the client's requirements regarding planning, scheduling, and program management should all be addressed within the RFP in as much detail as possible.

20.4.7　The number of operational items and anchor or linking items per form should be given if the procuring entity has already planned these details.

20.5　The RFP should specify the numbers of selected response items, constructed response or open-ended items (brief and extended), gridded response items, and essay items needed for the assessment.

20.5.1　For reading/language arts items that are passage-based, there should be a preference stated by the RFP authors for authentic, previously published stimulus passages or for commissioned, newly authored passages.

20.5.2　For mathematics items, there should be a preference stated for simple computation items that are not embedded in text versus text-based computation items, and for items that require the student to demonstrate different degrees of depth of knowledge, reasoning, and problem-solving.

20.5.3　For writing, modes of writing expected at each grade (e.g., descriptive, expository, narrative, persuasive) should be specified, and the type of scoring that is required (holistic, analytic, trait) should also be stated in the RFP. The presence or absence of selected response questions and testing mechanics of writing should be made clear. Examples of previous rubrics for scoring should be provided if new rubrics should be modeled after them.

20.5.4   For science, the RFP should specify the types of stimuli and the types of items that are expected. If any part of the science examination requires manipulatives or other experimental equipment, that also must be specified.

20.6   The composition and types of review committees should be specified in detail.

20.6.1   The number of persons and different types of persons (e.g., teachers, administrators, parents, technical experts, etc.) who will populate each committee should be specified.

20.6.2   The number of meetings for each committee and the duration of each meeting should be specified.

20.6.3   The successful service provider's responsibility for paying per diem amounts to each attendee, supplying food and/or refreshments or lodging, or paying honoraria must be specified.

20.6.4   The number and types of successful service provider staff who will either lead or provide support for each committee must be specified.

20.7   The measurement model for the assessment should be specified in the RFP.

20.7.1   Special requirements for verifying calibration, scaling, and equating should be specified in detail.

20.7.2   A technical specification should be included to indicate the level of detail that the state requires of a bidder/ service provider.

20.8   Each bidder will be responsible for producing a work schedule that will result in timely and accurate deliverables. To accomplish this, the RFP must provide a skeleton of the schedule with critical dates. These include:

- approximate dates of committee meetings;

- dates when materials must be delivered to districts or school sites;

- administration dates (or windows) during the year; and

- dates when student and group score report results need to be delivered to districts and schools.

20.8.1   If penalties or liquidated damages will be assessed for failure to meet the schedule or if the deliverables do not meet the requirements, penalties or liquidated damage amounts must be specified.

20.9   The RFP Cost Proposal will provide a standard document format that all bidders must use to display their costs.

20.9.1   The RFP authors should consider key information about costs that they need for decision-making and design the Cost Proposal document accordingly. The client's cost proposal forms should:

- be electronic;

- be formatted as a standardized cost submission spreadsheet;

- be at a level of detail that allows review of total costs;

- allow for cost elements that may be subject to adjustments;

- allow for elements that may be purchased individually or on an optional basis; and

- contain accuracy in the formulas.

20.9.2   If the unit price rather than the total price is required or allowed, there should be an explanation of how prices will be used and over what period of time they are required to be held constant.

20.9.3   The client should specify the N-count, including the minimum and maximum, so that comparable prices will be given by each bidder.

20.9.4   When appropriate, cost proposal forms should allow for fixed and variable unit costing.

20.10 The RFP should specify with reasonable detail the method that the state will use to evaluate the proposals and/or its various components (e.g., technical proposal, management plan, staffing, cost) to arrive at its decision. The RFP should comply with applicable procurement laws.

20.11 The RFP should specify the process by which bidders who feel that they may not have been treated fairly can protest the award decision and specify the procedures that will be applicable to any protest.

CHAPTER 21. TRANSITION FROM ONE SERVICE PROVIDER TO ANOTHER

Introduction

Continuation of the client's testing program should be of primary concern for the service providers involved in a contract transition. The transition between service providers should enable the testing program to continue with little interruption and few disruptions of service to the client, the client's stakeholders, and other persons that the client serves. It is necessary that the previous service provider, the client, and the new service provider maintain a cooperative and professional relationship to achieve the goal of a smooth and seamless transition. While the new service provider undoubtedly will have its own ideas about how to handle its responsibilities under the program, the first year of a new contract should be structured to minimize changes from the previous service provider in order to maintain the integrity of the longitudinal data and the consistency of score results. This continuity is particularly important in a high-stakes testing program. This chapter identifies some transitional procedures that have proven to be effective in successfully transferring from one service provider to another with little disruption to service.

21.1   **Management of the transition of materials, products, documents, and information will be the joint responsibility of the client, the previous service provider, and the new service provider. All materials and information should be provided, if possible, in an agreed-upon electronic format.**

   21.1.1   The parties involved in the transition—the client, the previous service provider, and the new service provider—should each name one person from their staff who will serve as transition point person. The named person should be responsible for the following:

   • communications within his or her own organization and between the other parties;

   • establishment of a positive, cooperative working relationship during the transition; and

- provision of electronic notification of materials being transferred (including both deliveries and receipts).

21.2 The client's responsibilities during the transition should include the following:

21.2.1 Expectations for the previous service provider and the new service provider should be communicated in writing to all persons involved in the transition.

21.2.2 Agreed-upon procedures and protocols should be established and enforced.

21.2.3 A timeline for deliverables should be maintained.

21.2.4 Records of materials being transferred should be maintained, including:

- a listing of transferable materials needed by new service provider;

- written assurance that the sent materials meet the new service provider's needs; and

- electronic record keeping of deliveries sent, received, completed, and still needed.

21.3 Meeting requirements will be coordinated by the parties to include the following:

21.3.1 Meetings with staff from the client, the previous service provider, and the new service provider should be scheduled. Those persons should include a named contact person for each entity and all key staff. Initial meetings should include a meeting of the entire group and smaller meetings organized by function areas. These meetings should produce the following:

- a timeline for transition work;

- a schedule for subsequent meetings;

- establishment of procedures and protocols; and

- a listing of all materials and files being transferred.

21.3.2   Face-to-face meetings may be conducted at set intervals during the transition, as needed. Meetings may be held for the entire group and for specific function areas.

21.3.3   Conference calls should be scheduled as needed between periodic face-to-face meetings. The purpose of these calls is to communicate the overall status of the transition, status of deliveries and receipts, and an updated timeline for the transition.

21.3.4   If requested by the client, the new service provider may attend any client-sponsored committee meetings (e.g. fairness/sensitivity, content advisory, test steering committees, and state TAC meetings) that occur during the transition period.

21.4   Copyright and permissions owned by the previous service provider may be transferred to the new service provider if they are specified in the contractual agreement with the client and the previous service provider. Copyright and permissions owned jointly by the client and the previous service provider should be transferred to the new service provider. Copyright and permissions owned by the client may be transferred to the new service provider if specified in the contractual agreement with the new service provider. Copyright and permission materials may include test questions, test stimuli, reading passages, test forms, and supplemental test materials.

21.5   Transfer of the item and test form information will be crucial to the maintenance of the testing program. All items and test forms owned by the client must be included in the transition of materials between service providers. A plan for the security of the transferred materials and data should be developed and implemented. Information that should be transferred includes the following:

- item specifications, test specifications, blueprints, style guides (for test forms, manuals, and test items), and test booklet layout specification, including embedded field-test items;

- established timelines for the assessment process from development to score reporting for all tests and all administrations;

- book maps and/or print-ready tests and key files for the next administration of the assessment, if the previous service provider is required to produce tests for next administration under the contract agreement;

- electronic versions in an agreed upon format (e.g., PDF or native file), complete with artwork, test books, special versions, and supplemental materials for all subjects and all administrations; and

- administration and development histories for all tests being transferred.

21.6 **Transfer of the client's item banks for all tests under the new service provider's contract will be a time-consuming process that requires attention to detail. Transfer of item banks should occur in a controlled, secure environment using an agreed upon electronic format, and should cover the following:**

- specifications for the item bank;

- all items and associated stimuli and graphics, checklists, and scoring guidelines used in assessments, including those designed as collections of evidence or portfolios;

- alignment information about items, passages, and tasks;

- parameters and attributes of items, stimuli, passages, and tasks;

- information and all related data about each item or task's current status, field-test administration, item position in test booklets, and any use in operational forms;

- approved but undeveloped reading passages, stimuli, and graphics, including source file; and

- all items ready for field testing.

21.7 The previous service provider and the client should provide information about special versions of all the assessments being transferred to the new service provider. This information may include the following:

- specifications for the Braille, large print, versions delivered in languages other than English, and bilingual versions;

- electronic and paper copies of each special version;

- prior year's administration production records, including information about numbers ordered and returned for scoring;

- any special instructions for ordering, handling, administration, returning materials, and special security procedures;

- description of the process for determining languages other than English to be tested and the number of special versions; and

- training materials for stakeholders.

21.8 The previous service provider will provide all contract-based, non-proprietary scoring information to the new service provider to maintain scoring consistency. This part of the transition between service providers may accommodate the exchange of all item-specific scoring materials so that the new service provider may replicate the scoring procedures of the previous service provider as required by the client. The information transferred should include the following:

21.8.1 Any information, existing agreements, and specifications that may be necessary for scanning.

21.8.2 The reader training materials with annotations for previous and ongoing administrations must be transferred, as well as materials for field-test items and operational items, including validation papers, training sets, and score anchor papers.

21.8.3   Field-test responses and/or range-finding materials for all items and tasks in item bank must also be transferred. (If the previous service provider is required to build test forms for next administration, all anchor papers, scoring materials, and training materials should be included in the materials given to the new service provider).

21.8.4   Details of established processes, and procedures, including:

- examples of special codes applied during scoring (e.g., non-scorables) for all items and tests;

- scoring specifications and rules for multiple choice, constructed response items and tasks;

- rules for scoring late batches, appeals, and tests returned with responses in languages other than English;

- rules for handling multiple answer documents that must be merged;

- rules for handling duplicate records; and

- scoring procedures, guidelines, and training materials for scoring at remote locations and/or by state groups.

21.9   **The new service provider should replicate the scoring of the previous service provider to establish equivalency of score results. The replication should include scanning, hand-scoring, score compilation, and score conversions.**

21.10   **Score reporting is most visible to the stakeholders, so it is important that there is consistency between the score reports produced by the previous and new service providers. The transition of score reports may include both paper and electronic transfer of the following:**

- itemized distribution lists and mock-ups of all reports, including family, teacher, principal, district, and state lists for all tests being transferred;

- interpretive guides for score reports;

- report specifications, business rules, decision rules, condition codes, and processing rules for all reports; and

- static and variable score report text.

21.11 A complete, seamless transfer of data files is essential for the archival of student records. Many entities are instituting longitudinal records for test takers where prior administration data will be crucial. Data files may be provided in a format agreed upon by both the previous and new service providers.

21.11.1 The files should include the following:

- the data from prior administrations including student data files and aggregated data for schools, districts, and states;

- contact information for districts, schools, test coordinators, committee members (fairness/ sensitivity, content, range finding, technical advisory, test steering, etc.), and college experts, if it is part of the contractual agreement;

- building and district ordering histories;

- a sample of the pre-code file used to print information on tests, answer documents, or labels; and

- layout specifications for all data files.

21.11.2 Relevant information for dealing with data and data files may be provided to the new service provider by either the client or the previous service provider. That information should include:

- data review guidelines including statistical flags and review procedures; and

- business rules and specifications.

21.12 Records of the process history and technical adequacy of the assessment system maintained by the previous service provider should be transferred to the new service provider. Technical reports should be provided in electronic form, if possible, for all assessments that are being transitioned. The reports being transferred may include:

- previous technical reports;

- standard setting reports;

- alignment reports;

- calibration and equating reports;

- vertical scaling reports;

- research reports providing validity evidence; and

- Technical Advisory Committee records/presentations.

21.13 Technical specifications for each assessment should include:

- any data analysis and checks required of the service provider by the client;

- rules for combining readers' scores on free response items; and

- rounding rules for raw scores (if applicable) and for scale scores.

21.14 Supplemental materials and documents related to the assessment system, including practice tests, whether in electronic and paper formats, must be transferred.

21.14.1 The previous service provider should provide the following to the new service provider for each practice test:

- duplication-ready Braille files and large print files;

- extra printed copies of each test as well as extra copies of the Braille and large print versions;

- extra CD or video copies of tests delivered in languages other than English and English language versions;

- copies of translation and read-aloud scripts;

- scoring papers, keys, and score conversion tables; and

- manuals and support materials needed for each test and special version.

21.15 Any existing form or letter text that the client has approved for use should be supplied to the new service provider in electronic form. These may include:

- data forms released between or within educational entities including:

    – between school entities, if appropriate;

    – within the educational hierarchy; and

    – between educational service providers;

- protocols, procedures, policies, and practices;

- answer documents, mock-ups, and specifications; and

- memos accompanying reports, shipments, and test materials returned.

21.16 Any existing inventory of test materials paid for by the client and intended to be used by the new service provider must be transferred. These materials may include calculators used during the test, manipulatives, and booklets, as well as pamphlets, flyers, etc., used to inform stakeholders about the tests.

21.17 If the transition includes the transfer of a support website housed by the previous service provider, then it should be transferred to the new service provider if it is owned by the client. The format of the electronic transfer should be agreed upon by the previous and new service providers.

- all resources, text, and items, including supporting materials, and art for the website;

- organizational structure of any professional development tools; and

- any templates and HTML text surrounding the templates.

21.18 The change from the previous service provider to the new service provider may occur during a test administration. If so, the following information should be transferred between the two service providers:

- book maps and answer keys for tests;

- electronic copies of the tests;

- order and shipping files, including additional or late orders;

- sample return kit, if appropriate;

- enrollment information used to print answer documents or student labels;

- secure materials files; and

- conversion tables to be used in test equating.

21.19 Transition services should be covered in the scope of the contract either through the initial RFP or through a change order. The client should specify which services need to be covered.

GLOSSARY OF TERMS

Introduction

- **Best practices**
  A set of practices that, when applied, yield high-quality, repeatable outcomes for a variety of operational functions.

Chapter 1

- **Client**
  An entity which contracts for services. When applied in the large-scale assessment market, the client is typically a state department of education.

- **Service provider**
  An entity which provides services to clients. When applied in the large-scale assessment market, service providers contracting directly with clients are typically considered prime contractors. Service providers contracting with prime contractors to provided components of the overall contract are typically considered subcontractors.

- **LEA**
  Local Education Agency, which may consist of any local entity that reports to a state organization and with which either a client or its contractor may need to communicate about local implementation of a state's large-scale assessment program. These entities are typically districts, systems, or schools.

Chapter 2

- **Test design**
  This fundamentally defines the nature of a test. Test design may include information about the number of questions, formats of questions, desired layouts, use of supporting materials, and other aspects which affect how the test is administered.

- **Test curriculum blueprint**
  This is the coverage of the curriculum frameworks and benchmarks within an assessment, often manifested as a percentage of test questions per content standard or benchmark.

- **Item development plan**
  This is the process for the development of test questions, typically including item prototypes, definitions of item development specifications, item review procedures, schedules, quantities, and quality acceptance criteria.

- **Item specifications**
  These are the defining factors of individual items, typically including content tested, item types, cognitive complexity, rigor of items, reading passage levels, and use of graphics, tables, and charts.

- **Bias review**
  A review of an individual test item that identifies potential bias toward one or more defined populations.

- **Editorial review**
  A review of a test item that identifies and corrects grammatical issues.

- **Scoring rubrics**
  An established set of criteria, including rules, principles, keys, and illustrations, used to determine a student's performance on an assessment task, constructed-response item, or multiple choice item.

- **Foil distributions**
  Summaries of the number of correct answers for each of the response categories in a multiple choice response test. Where "A, B, C, etc." are used to label response choices, how many correct answers are "A's", how many "B's" etc. Foil distributions are used to check that there are not unusual numbers of a particular response being used as the correct answer.

- **Quartile analysis**
  Consists of establishing three points (defined as low, middle, or upper) which divide the scores in a distribution into four equal groups, each containing 25% of the data. Quartiles are special cases of percentiles – the lower, middle, and upper quartiles correspond to the 25th, 50th (median), and 75th percentiles.

- **Biserial, point-biserial, item-to-total correlation data**
  These terms represent the traditional measures of how well a test item is able to differentiate between top performers and low performers on a test. These statistics are all typically variations on the correlation coefficient and generally yield high values when the item is able to distinguish between responses of top performers and low performers on the test.

- **P-value / Item mean**
  The p-value is the mathematical average of item performance when the item is dichotomous (e.g., multiple choice). In this case, the p-value is also the percentage of students selecting the correct answer. When the item is polytomous (e.g., multiple response categories) the item average or item mean is the simple average of student scores. Traditionally the p-value and item mean have been indices of item difficulty.

- **Theta value**
  Estimate of the relationship between a test item and the underlying attribute that is being measured. A distinction is made between the values that are actually obtained in a test setting and a hypothesized "true" underlying value.

- **DIF (Differential Item Functioning)**
  A statistical property of a test item in which different groups of test-takers who have the same total test score have different average item scores.

Chapter 3

- **Meta-data**
  Meta-data is the term used to represent all information associated with a test question other than the question itself. For example, information such as the font size, the formatting, the statistics, the value or weight of the item, the correct response key, which content standard the item measures, etc., are meta-data.

- **CAT (Computer Adaptive Test)**
  A computer adaptive test is one in which the next test question is selected (and typically administered) by a computer algorithm based on the student's performance on previously administered items. In such a way, an assessment can be tailored to the individual based on how he or she responds, thereby adding precision to the resulting scores since the student only sees the test questions most appropriate for him or her.

- **CBT (Computer-Based Test)**
  A computer-based test is one where technology presents what would otherwise be a traditional paper test form to the students. As such, the students are taking the same assessment as those seeing a paper version but are doing so on a computer.

- **Transadaptation**
  This is the process by which a test is translated and adapted for use in a different language and often a different cultural context from the one in which the test was originally developed. Professional standards usually require that such translations or adaptations must be separately validated from the original test, at least where it is feasible to do so (e.g., where a sufficient sample size exists for such validation).

- **Item cluster**
  An item cluster is a group of items (often measuring common content) that may provide a separate score. For example, a group of items all measuring whole number addition might represent an item cluster.

- **Cloned items**
  Cloned items are items that are generated to appear and function like a specific item. For example, a two digit whole-number addition question like $12 + 34 = X$ has many clones: $34 + 12 = X$; $44 + 2 = X$ and so on. Test builders must be careful that the prevalence and use of clones are understood in order to avoid any unanticipated consequences from their use.

- **Item positioning**
  Item positioning refers to the serial location in the assessment in which an item is placed. This could be relative to the beginning of the assessment, beginning of a section (i.e., after a break) or both. Item positioning is of paramount importance when moving a test question from field testing to live testing, as context effects and fatigue due to different positions might impact performance.

- **Field test / Pilot test / Item tryout**
  These are terms applied to the collection of item and test level performance necessary to build and support live or operational test forms. These testings might include the embedding of newly-developed items for data collection within an operational test form, stand-alone testing of newly-developed items, or small scale classroom testing where informal information about the performance of the items or assessment is collected.

- **XML (Extensible Markup Language)**
  XML is an open technology standard defining how documents are formatted and exchanged electronically. This standard allows for the exchange of documents and information electronically not only via the internet but also across various software technologies and platforms.

- **PDF (Portable Document Format)**
  PDF is a proprietary standard owned by Adobe Systems for the generation and formatting of documents. This standard allows for the exchange of documents across technologies.

Chapter 4

- **Matrix sampling**
  Dividing up a collection of test materials so that different test-takers get different subsets of test questions and no one test-taker takes all the questions that are being administered. Matrix sampling permits covering a great amount of content for the group of test-takers without unduly burdening any one individual. The National Assessment of Educational Progress uses matrix sampling to test large amounts of material without requiring very long time blocks from any one participant.

- **Ancillary manipulatives**
  These include items such as rulers, protractors, and any other non-standard items needed to be able to answer certain questions on a test. These are usually used on math or science tests and often are associated with a unit of measure.

- **Demographic data**
  Data associated with a student, including such things as last name, first name, birth date, identification numbers, ethnicity, gender, ELL, ESL, free/reduced lunch, and any accommodations needed. The data can be collected through pre-identification processes or on answer documents. The data are used for reporting purposes, including the disaggregation of student subgroups (see definition in Chapter 17).

Chapter 5

- **Sampling specifications**
  These specifications define the rules for collecting a sample. Typically this requires definition of the population from which the sample is drawn, the characteristics or parameters used in selecting the sample (such as geographic region, manufacturing facility, or production lot), the size of the sample, instructions regarding how missing or declining cases are handled, and requirements for describing the accuracy and representativeness of the sample once drawn.

Chapter 6

- **Enrollment data**
  The number of students enrolled within a state or LEA, typically provided by class and/or grade, school, and district. Enrollment data are used to calculate quantities of test materials to be produced and shipped to each location.

- **Overage requirements**
  Overage requirements refer to the number of extra test materials to be sent to schools and/or districts. Administrators use this overage to provide test materials for students who were not part of the enrollment data compiled prior to test administration.

- **Secure materials**
  Assessments and test materials that must be protected from release prior to test administration or because they will be reused in the future. In the context of large-scale assessments, some contracts require that any proprietary intellectual property or other confidential information be returned in their entirety to the party who owns them so that they can be accounted for.

- **Spiral**
  Developing multiple versions of a test booklet or computer-based test where one or more sections vary from test-taker to test-taker. The term is also used to describe a process where different test booklets are given to test-takers at the same test site. For example, if there were five different variants (Version 1, Version 2, etc.), every sixth test-taker would receive Version 1, and so on. Spiraling can be used to get data on several different sets of test items or as a security measure to minimize the chance that test-takers sitting adjacent to or immediately in front of or behind each other will have the same test booklet. Operationally, spiraling refers to how the forms will be collated so that a test administrator can hand the tests out in order rather than trying to mix the forms at time of test administration.

- **Breach form**
  Another form of the test which will be held in reserve in case security is breached on any other forms. The breach form can then be administered as a secure form.

- **Barcode**
  A standardized image containing a series of parallel lines with an associated number, which can be read by an optical scanner. Barcodes and their numbers are associated with a set of data resident in a data file or data warehouse. In assessment, pre-identification barcodes are tied to student demographic data, and security barcodes are tied to the location where the secure document was distributed.

Chapter 7

- **Scope of work (SOW)**
  An attachment to a contract between two parties specifically identifying the work each party will fulfill.

- **Service level agreement (SLA)**
  An attachment to a contract between two parties specifically identifying the timing, level or other similar functionality to which work will be completed. SLAs typically set timeframes (e.g., turnaround and response time) and quality levels.

- **Confidentiality agreement**
  An agreement between two parties identifying how information that is considered confidential is to be treated when shared between the parties and what terms of liability will apply to any violation of such confidentiality requirements. These are often interchangeable with nondisclosure agreements.

- **Nondisclosure agreement**
  An agreement between two parties that stipulates that confidential information shared between the two parties will not be disclosed to any third party or even within the entity to which the information has been disclosed, as well as how such information is to be used and returned to the party who owns the information. These are often interchangeable with confidentiality agreements.

Chapter 8

- **Encrypted data exchange**
  Encoding data so that only those with a key to translate the code can

read the data. Often student-identifiable data and other confidential information being shared via electronic means (internet) will be encrypted so that the data cannot be obtained even if someone were to hack into the database or the transmission of the data.

- **Secure FTP/FTPS (File Transfer Protocol and FTP Sites)** Locations to which secure materials can be sent using a secure communications protocol with relative confidence that the material will not be compromised. Access to the site is limited to approved users with active passwords and the site is not connected to the internet and is maintained separately and protected by firewall from others who have access to material on the same server, but not the Secure FTP site.

Chapter 9

- **Timing study** A timing study is typically a research study ascertaining the amount of time required for a test administration. A timing study may include analyses of field test information regarding perceptions of student time-on-task, duration of directions and set up as well as collection of test materials. A timing study may also look at omit rates, completion rates or other artifacts of operational testing. The goal of any such timing investigation is to help ensure that adequate or anticipated time is allowed for administration of an assessment.

- **District Assessment Coordinator** The person responsible for managing the assessment program for the LEA or district. This is the single point contact and/or authority representing the district in the assessment system. This person will coordinate with the service provider or the State Department regarding aspects of the assessment system.

- **Building Assessment Coordinator** The person responsible for managing the assessment program at each assessment site or school building. This is the single point contact and/or authority representing the test administration site and will coordinate closely with the District Assessment Coordinator.

- **Testing environment** The testing environment means the general physical surroundings at the time of testing. Aspects of lighting, noise, heating, furniture are part of the testing environment and need to be controlled such that all students have the best testing experience possible. The testing environment also is standardized so that all students have the same testing experience.

- **PDA (Personal Digital Assistant)**
  PDAs are electronic devices students might use to interfere with the testing environment. Examples include cell phones, iPod's, recorders, calendars, e-book readers, etc.

- **Collusion**
  Any planned or collaborated manipulation or variance in standardized testing protocol between two or more students/administrators. Collusion could be as simple as two students cheating or a more elaborate scheme involving many students and/or administrators that leads to inappropriate test administrations and the need to decide whether test scores have been compromised.

- **Security breach**
  Any activity that leads to a uncontained exposure (i.e., outside of the testing environment) of secure testing materials, including test content, directions or other secure testing artifacts that adversely affects the integrity and validity of the assessment.

- **Segment**
  A specific subset of the assessment typically administered in one sitting.

Chapter 10

- **Packing list**
  A report identifying how materials are packed for shipment and the location of specific materials in specific boxes. This report accompanies shipments of materials prior to administration.

- **Ancillary materials**
  Ancillary materials include all supporting materials other than actual student tests. Examples include packing lists, directions for administration, security checking lists, return packaging lists, etc.

- **Lot sampling**
  This is a procedure where samples of materials are taken and verified against a master list or source. For example, a "lot" could be one classroom packaged within a school and

district shipment. The actual contents of this "lot" are then verified against what is supposed to be in the lot.

Chapter 11

- **Chain of custody**
  An unbroken written trail of accountability records related to tracking of testing materials being handed off from one service provider to another or to the client, or between the client and the district/school personnel, to ensure that no inappropriate activity has taken place that could affect test security.

- **Proofs**
  Prior to printing materials, a print vendor will provide a proof as a representation of what it will print and collate. The proof is then checked against specifications to ensure that the printed materials are what is expected and an approval of the proof is given to the printer to proceed to finish the job.

- **Shipper**
  Any stakeholder who sends materials to another stakeholder.

- **Transporter**
  Any provider of transportation services between stakeholders.

- **Receiver**
  Any stakeholder who receives test materials from another stakeholder.

Chapter 12

- **Header sheet**
  Header sheets are used to collect data from populations into the correct groupings. Header sheets are scanned with all answer documents within a grouping to ensure data are collected accurately for future group reports. Groups might include grade, class, and building.

Chapter 13

- **Anchor points**
  Set points on a scannable page that allow an image to be aligned so that a mark's location can be read in relation to the anchor points.

- **Timing tracks**
  In OMR (Optical Mark Reader) scanning, timing tracks are the boxes along the side of a scannable page to which bubbles align.

- **Dropout ink**
  Ink that drops out of a scanned image leaving only the marks from the test-taker.

- **Multiple marks**
  On a gridded multiple choice answer document, one question having two answers marked with similar intensities so that the intent of the test-taker cannot be determined.

- **Incomplete marks**
  On a gridded multiple choice answer document, marks that do not fully fill in the bubble and result in manual determination of whether the answer may be scored.

- **Light marks**
  On a gridded multiple choice answer document, marks that are too light in intensity so that the question is determined to be unanswered.

- **Erasures**
  On a gridded multiple choice answer document, a test-taker may erase one answer and mark another. Erasures may often result in light marks.

- **Nonconforming marks**
  On a gridded multiple choice answer document, marks that do not fully fill in a grid space and result in manual determination of whether the answer may be scored.

- **Test deck**
  A service provider's quality assurance group will bubble answer documents with all available marks and different intensities. These answer documents will then be scanned, and the data collected checked to ensure that the scanners are collecting data from the answer documents as expected.

- **User acceptance test**
  A test performed by the user to ensure that software is working as the user intended.

- **Litho code**
  A code on a scannable answer document specific to each individual answer document. This allows for multiple page answer documents to be brought back together in case individual sheets are mixed.

- **Editing process**
  After scanning, a process will be followed to ensure that the data collected from an answer document is identical to how a human would collect it. This process also allows for humans to check that any blank fields in the data file match up with unread marks or fields not bubbled on the answer document.

- **Acclimatized**
  Based on humidity and the amount of moisture in the paper, sheets can shrink or expand causing marks to move on the page. Scannable documents should be kept in a climate controlled area for an appropriate amount of time prior to scanning to ensure that marks have not moved.

- **Calibration**
  Scanners occasionally need to be calibrated to ensure that all sheets are read consistently.

- **Flatbed**
  When sheets cannot be scanned on high-speed scanners, images are sometimes captured on desktop image scanners (flatbed scanners) so that an electronic version is captured.

- **Key entry**
  When a sheet cannot be scanned, it can be sent to a person to enter the data from the sheet into the data file.

Chapter 14

- **Range finding**
  In hand scoring, a process used to find a range of student responses articulating acceptable performance as defined by a scoring rubric and/or score point category.

- **Anchor papers**
  These are collections of papers that demonstrate a range of score values from sample student responses to a constructed-response item. They serve as the quintessential responses expected and have been identified by the client to serve as representative scoring of the item against the scoring rubric. All other scored items are to be scored

against the expectations and justifications established in the anchor papers.

- **Validity papers/check sets**
  These are papers of actual student work with known score values (typically assigned or agreed upon by expert scorers) that are then seeded within actual scoring work (unbeknown to the scorers) for the purpose of verifying their scoring accuracy.

- **Read behind**
  A process where one or more secondary expert scorers read student responses to help ensure that initial scorers have assigned accurate scores.

- **Inter-rater reliability**
  An agreement index that measures the consistency between any two or more scorers that assigned scores on the same free-response (i.e. constructed-respose items) items.

- **Adjudication**
  The process used to resolve scores resulting from human scorers that do not agree within some defined criteria.

- **Disturbing content**
  Content contained within a student's response that constitutes an immediate and potential threat of harm, violence, abuse or illegal activity that should be investigated further.

Chapter 15

- **CBT (Computer-Based Test)**
  See definition contained in Chapter 3.

- **Drivers**
  Software required in order to make technical devices (e.g., printers) function properly.

- **LAN (Local Area Network)**
  A technology-based (i.e., electronic) linking of two or more computers together using a local communications network environment (as compared to a WAN, or wide area network).

- **FAQs (Frequently Asked Questions)**
  A list of most frequently asked questions or questions anticipated by users of the device, technology, software or procedure.

- **Latency**
  Delays typically measured in clock time.

Chapter 16

- **Technical defensibility**
  This is the evidence that the assessment follows the professional technical standards jointly developed and published by the American Educational Research Association, the American Psychological Association, and the National Council of Measurement in Education.

- **Reliability**
  The consistency of scores resulting from an assessment.

- **Validity**
  The accuracy of inferences made using the scores resulting from an assessment.

- **Standard setting**
  A subjective procedure based on a reasonable determination of the performance by user for setting cut scores on an assessment.

- **Equating**
  The statistical linking of scores on one or more assessments.

- **Alignment**
  Traditionally refers to the degree of agreement between the content measured on an assessment and the content standards and benchmarks required in the curriculum.

- **Field test sampling**
  A process for representative selection of students to respond to questions that do not yet count for the purpose of evaluating the performance of these items prior to placing them on a live assessment.

- **Disaggregated data**
  Data summarized by grouping various breakout categories, such as gender, grade, subtest, etc. (see definition of student subgroups in Chapter 17).

- **Parameter estimates**
  Estimates of the statistical values associated with test questions, such as difficulty and discrimination.

- **Vertical scale**
  A single standardized reporting system allowing for comparison of scores across grades.

Chapter 17

- **Report design**
  Physical layout of the score report.

- **Reporting specification**
  Requirements of the report (i.e., what information the report will contain and how it should be formatted).

- **Interpretation guide**
  Additional information regarding how to interpret data on the score reports.

- **Decision rules**
  Rules and requirements for how a decision will be made.

- **Parent/Guardian reports**
  Score reports customized to convey information to student's parents or guardians.

- **Class rosters**
  A list report showing the most pertinent information for the entire class in an efficient space.

- **School/District consolidated reports**
  Reports that provide both school and district information together on one report.

- **Student subgroups**
  Groupings required in section 1111(b)(3)(C)(xiii) of the ESEA (i.e., by gender, by each major racial and ethnic group, by English proficiency status, by migrant status, by students with disabilities as compared to nondisabled students, and by economically disadvantaged students as compared to students who are not economically disadvantaged, except that such aggregation is not required in a case in which the number of students in a subgroup is insufficient to yield statistically reliable information or the results would reveal personally identifiable information about an individual student).

Chapter 18

- **Key**
  Indication of the correct answer for a multiple choice test question.

- **DOB (Date of Birth)**
  Student birth date.

- **FTP/FTPS (File Transfer Protocol and FTP Site)**
  See definition contained in Chapter 8.

- **SIS (Student Information System)**
  The information management system, software, or database containing school and/or district information about students.

- **Mock data**
  Simulated data in the correct format and value range as real data resulting from an assessment which is created as a tool to check aspects of the assessment system.

Chapter 19

- **Special populations**
  Test-takers who may require accommodations to the core assessments used by all students. These may include students with special needs, English-language learners, students with physical handicaps, etc.

- **Accommodations**
  Changes in the administration of an assessment, including but not limited to changes in assessment setting, scheduling, timing, presentation format, response mode, and combinations of these changes, that do not change the construct intended to be measured by the assessment or the meaning of the resulting scores. Accommodations must be used for equity in assessment and not provide advantage to students eligible to receive them.

- **Universal design**
  A set of assessment construction principles that seeks to maximize accessibility of the assessment for all students by avoiding content that may create distractions or irrelevancies for some test-takers, especially those who fall within a special population.

Chapter 20

- **N-count**
  Number of students.

- **Anchor/linking items**
  Items used in an assessment to link statistically scores on two different forms of a test across grades or between different administrations.

- **Manipulatives**
  Materials required for test-takers to answer the assessment questions. Examples of manipulatives include: rulers, protractors, pictures, scratch paper, and calculators.

Chapter 21

- **Item specifications**
  See definition contained in Chapter 2.

- **Test specifications**
  Test specifications are specific rules and characteristics that guide the development of a test's content and format. They indicate what content will be assessed on the test and in what proportions.

- **Test curriculum blueprint**
  See definition contained in Chapter 2.

- **Style guide**
  A style guide serves to clarify issues of how to write items for a client's assessments. Its intended audiences are item writers and material production staff (if the style guide addresses the construction of test format). Item review committees may also reference the style guide during their deliberations from time to time.

- **Book map**
  A book map identifies the manner in which test items will be positioned in a form to be administered to students.

- **Operational item**
  A test question that will be used to contribute to the students score; a "live" item.

- **Field test item**
  A test question (often embedded within the operational items) that is inserted to obtain statistical information about its performance and ability to measure its intended content; this item does not count toward the student score but its data are used for future test development.

- **Validation papers**
  Sets of pre-scored student papers used to ensure that a scorer of constructed-response items is able to assign scores to items within an acceptable range of consistency; these papers are typically inserted into operational scoring to ensure scorers maintain their consistency during the scoring process.

- **Training sets**
  These are collections of pre-scored student papers used specifically to train human scorers as they prepare to assign scores to constructed-response items.

- **Anchor papers**
  See definition contained in Chapter 14.

- **Late batches**
  These are scoreable materials, usually from a school or district, that arrive after the deadline required by the client. These materials often have to be handled separately in a manner that may delay the inclusion of their results in aggregate reporting.

- **Appeal**
  A request by a school or district on behalf of a student where the official score derived from the assessment is challenged as to its accuracy.

- **Duplicate record**
  An instance when two identical or similarly coded answer documents are returned to a service provider. A hierarchy of which record takes precedence must be established.

- **Condition code**
  Labels assigned to student results that identify the conditions that have been met during the scoring process (e.g., valid score, not attempted, incomplete).

- **Free-response item**
  An item that – unlike a multiple choice item – allows the student to construct or generate a response to the item.

- **Read-aloud script**
  A script that is provided for a test administrator that is then read to students in its exact format by the test administrator.

7331841R0

Made in the USA
Lexington, KY
12 November 2010